# easy good food

# easy good food

**Clare Ferguson** with photography by **Peter Cassidy** and **Jeremy Hopley**

RYLAND
PETERS
& SMALL

LONDON  NEW YORK

Senior Designer **Catherine Randy**
Commissioning Editor
**Elsa Petersen-Schepelern**
Production **Deborah Wehner**
Art Director **Gabriella Le Grazie**
Publishing Director **Alison Starling**

Food Stylist **Clare Ferguson**
Assistant Food Stylists **Fiona Smith,
Bethany Heald, Pippa Cuthbert**
Stylist **Wei Tang**

Photographers **Peter Cassidy**
Pages 2, 4, 5, 6, 7, 8 left, 10, 11, 18, 19, 28, 29, 32,
33, 38, 40 –41, 42–43, 45, 46, 48 right, 49, 50, 51,52,
53, 54, 54, 57, 58, 59, 62, 67, 72 right, 73 left, 75, 79,
83, 90, 91, 93, 94, 97, 98, 101, 103, 104, 105, 107,
108, 109, 112–113, 119, 120, 125, 126 left, 127 left,
132, 138, 139, 140, 141, Endpapers.
**Jeremy Hopley**
Pages 1, 3, 8 right, 9, 12–13, 15, 17, 21, 22–23,
24–25, 27, 30, 34, 37, 48 left, 60, 65, 68, 71, 72 left,
73 right, 76, 80–81, 85, 86–87, 89, 110, 114–115, 116,
122–123, 126 right, 127 right, 129, 131, 135, 136.

First published in Great Britain in 2002
by Ryland Peters & Small
Kirkman House,
12–14 Whitfield Street
London  W1T 2RP
www.rylandpeters.com

Text © Clare Ferguson 2002
Design and photographs
© Ryland Peters & Small 2002

Printed in China

10 9 8 7 6 5 4 3 2 1

ISBN 1 84172 250 2

A CIP record for this book is available from
the British Library.

**AUTHOR'S ACKNOWLEDGEMENTS**
My warmest thanks to Fiona Lindsay and
Linda Shanks of Limelight Management,
Fiona Smith, Pippa Cuthbert and Bethany
Heald, my able assistants, and Christine
Boodle of Better Read. Thanks also to
Paola, and to my favourite Notting Hill
suppliers; David Lidgate of C. Lidgate,
Butchers and Charcutiers, Haydn and Philip
of Kingsland, the Edwardian Butchers,
Mr Christian's Deli, Chalmers and Gray,
fishmongers, Michanicou Brothers,
greengrocers, Speck, Italian Deli and to the
cheerful stallholders of Portobello Road.

Though I am grateful for the advice, opinions
and expertise of those mentioned, any
imperfections in these pages must be my
responsibility, not theirs.

Recipes from this book have been published
previously in *Chicken: from Maryland to Kiev,
Extra Virgin: Cooking with Olive Oil, Flavours
of China, Flavours of Mexico, Flavours of Italy,
Street Food* and *Rice: from Risotto to Sushi*
all by Clare Ferguson.

**DEDICATION**
To Ian, my husband, with love and thanks.

**NOTES**
All spoon measurements used in this book
are level unless otherwise specified.

Uncooked or partly cooked eggs should not
be served to the very old or frail, the very
young or to pregnant women.

Ovens should be preheated to the specified
temperature. Recipes in this book were
tested with a regular oven. If using a fan-
assisted oven, decrease the oven
temperature by 20°C (40°F), or follow the
manufacturer's instructions.

# contents

Are you short of time, but still want to cook good things? Remember, good fresh food, quickly cooked, can take less time than heating up a pre-cooked ready-meal from the supermarket. These are my favourite easy recipes. Some are perfect for quick family meals, some are more spectacular for a special dinner and some make perfect party food.

# Easy good food …

What makes cooking relaxed and fun is having confidence and enjoying the whole process – getting a lively food idea, shopping, preparing and cooking it effectively, serving the dish with pride and, finally, eating it with pleasure.

How do we make every snack, every meal, effortless and good? I start with a storecupboard of basics that allows me to add spice, verve and flavour to other dishes. Staples like rice, noodles and pasta are important – I keep several kinds of each on hand. I buy my favourite spices in small quantities (they lose their flavour over time). I also keep special treats, like dried mushrooms, canned anchovies, sun-dried tomatoes and peppers, all of which allow me to give some kick to my cooking. I also keep virgin olive oil, capers, curry pastes and hot sauces, plus cans of tuna, coconut milk, chickpeas and beans such as cannellini, red kidney and borlotti beans to save time soaking the dried ones from scratch.

I don't have a freezer chock-full of ready-meals, but it does contain wonton wrappers, filo pastry, Asian flavourings such as kaffir lime leaves, lemongrass, grated ginger, even chillies, so I don't have to visit an Asian market every week. Frozen berries, ice cream and flatbreads are brilliant, too.

Back-up ingredients like these make life easy – but, for food to be good, it must also be fresh. Buying food fresh allows you to control the quality of what you buy. I make sure my meat, poultry and eggs are all free-range and organic. My fish is always fresh from a proper fishmonger. Fruit, vegetables and herbs are better when bought in small quantities often – their vitamins and other nutrients are more viable and better for you when used fresh or freshly cooked.

Given good basic ingredients, cooking doesn't have to be difficult. For this reason I decided to collect many of my best, easiest recipes and put them into this one, user-friendly cookbook *Easy Good Food*. Have fun cooking – and eat well, too.

# starters

# & snacks

Some people think frying in oil is difficult, but it couldn't be easier. I use a good-quality oil because it's healthier – olive oil is great, but others like peanut, sunflower or safflower oil are also good. Make the batter first, then set aside while you prepare the vegetables.

# vegetable fritto misto

**4 courgettes, sliced into thin ribbons with a vegetable peeler**

**8 baby spinach leaves**

**8 sprigs of flat leaf parsley**

**8 spring onions, halved crossways**

**8 baby asparagus spears**

**8 okra, stalk ends trimmed slightly**

**olive oil or peanut oil, for deep-frying**

**2 limes or lemons, cut into wedges, to serve (optional)**

BATTER

**250 g plain flour**

**3 tablespoons olive oil**

**3 egg whites**

**¼ teaspoon salt**

**SERVES 4–6**

Wash and dry all the vegetables with kitchen paper. If using okra, trim the stalk ends only, so none of the interior is exposed.

To make the batter, sift the flour into a large bowl. Put the olive oil into a second bowl, add 350 ml warm water and beat well. Beat the oil mixture into the sifted flour to give a creamy batter, then set aside for about 20 minutes.

Meanwhile pour about 10 cm depth of oil into a deep-fryer or a saucepan fitted with a chip basket. Heat the oil to 200°C (400°F) or until a cube of bread browns in about 25 seconds.

Put the egg whites and salt into a separate straight-sided bowl, whisk well, then fold the mixture gently through the batter.

Using tongs or a skewer, dip each piece of vegetable into the batter, then fry in batches until crisp, golden and vividly green. Remove and drain on crumpled kitchen paper and keep hot while you fry the remaining vegetables. Serve hot with lime or lemon wedges, if using.

Put the chilli flakes, salt and orange zest into a bowl and toss gently. Put the oil into a medium saucepan or electric deep-fryer and heat to 190°C (375°F).

To peel the plantains, cut off the ends and run the tip of a sharp knife down the length of the plantain 2–3 times. Push your fingertips between the skin and the flesh and pull off the skin. Slice the plantain into long, thin strips using a mandoline or vegetable peeler.

Working in batches, put the strips into a frying basket and deep-fry until golden and crisp. Remove from the oil and drain on crumpled kitchen paper. While still hot, toss in the chilli, salt and orange mixture.

To make the salsa, either stir the ingredients together in a bowl, or purée very briefly with a food processor or mortar and pestle – the texture should be very coarse. Spoon over the chips or use as a dipping sauce.

**2 teaspoons dried chilli flakes**

**2 teaspoons sea salt flakes**

**2 teaspoons finely grated orange zest**

**1 litre peanut or corn oil, for frying**

**2 green plantains or 3 large green bananas**

MANGO SALSA

**1 medium-hot red chilli, such as Fresno, jalapeño, Anaheim or poblano, roasted, skinned, deseeded and sliced**

**½–1 serrano chilli (red or green), sliced**

**1 medium mango, peeled, seed removed and flesh finely diced**

**½ papaya, peeled, deseeded and diced**

**1 small red onion, finely diced**

**juice of 2 limes**

**juice of 1 orange**

**2 tablespoons light soy sauce**

**2 garlic cloves, chopped**

**2 teaspoons caster sugar**

**SERVES 4 AS A SNACK**

# spicy plantain crisps
## with chilli mango salsa

Plantains are cooking bananas – if you can't find them, use green bananas, sweet potatoes or parsnips. Thinly slice the flesh lengthways using a mandoline or vegetable peeler so they curl into long loops.

# shoestring french fries
## with homemade mayonnaise

**about 500 ml homemade mayonnaise, to serve (page 43)**

**1 kg floury potatoes***

**olive oil and peanut oil, mixed, for frying**

**sea salt and freshly ground black pepper**

**SERVES 4**

*Potatoes fall into two categories; waxy and floury. Floury potatoes are best for baking and deep-frying, and are often labelled as such. They will produce a crisp exterior and a fluffy interior.

Homemade French fries or potato chips are easy to make, taste great and are better for you than most takeaway varieties. I prefer to use olive oil, because it is the healthiest option with the best flavour, but peanut oil – also known as groundnut or arachide oil – is good, because it is virtually tasteless. The secret to good chips is to cook them twice.

Make the mayonnaise according to the recipe on page 43.

To make the fries, cut the potatoes lengthways into 5 mm slices, then cut the slices crossways to make 5 mm matchsticks. Put into a bowl of iced water. When ready to cook, drain and pat very dry on kitchen paper or a clean cloth.

Fill a saucepan or deep-fryer one-third full of oil and heat to 190°C (375°F) or until a cube of bread browns in 30 seconds. Half-fill a frying basket with the matchstick potatoes, lower into the oil and cook until light-brown, about 4 minutes. Remove and drain on crumpled kitchen paper. Repeat until all the potatoes have been cooked.

Skim and reheat the oil to the same temperature. Add the potatoes and cook a second time until very crisp, about 2 minutes. Remove, drain and keep hot. Repeat until all are cooked. Sprinkle with salt and pepper and serve with the mayonnaise.

The Spanish tortilla is a chunky omelette, thick with potatoes, onions and red peppers. Like all omelettes, it's simplicity itself. Serve it as a substantial lunch dish or cut it into cubes and serve as finger food at a party. Everyone loves it – and it's a great way to please all the vegetarians in the group.

**4 tablespoons extra virgin olive oil, preferably Spanish**

**750 g potatoes, halved lengthways and thickly sliced**

**2–3 Spanish onions, about 500 g, sliced**

**1 red pepper, cored and diced (optional)**

**6 eggs**

**sea salt flakes and freshly ground black pepper**

**SERVES 6–8**

# spanish potato tortilla

Heat 2 tablespoons of the oil in a large, heavy-based frying pan. Add the potatoes, onions and pepper, if using, and sauté over medium heat for 25–30 minutes or until tender, covering the pan for the last 10 minutes, stirring occasionally.

Put the eggs, salt and pepper into a bowl and lightly beat with a fork. Using a slotted spoon, transfer the potato mixture into the bowl and stir briefly.

Add 1 tablespoon of the oil to the pan and heat until very hot. Quickly pour in the egg and potato mixture and reduce the heat to medium. Leave the omelette to cook, undisturbed, until the base is deep golden and firm, about 5–6 minutes.

Slide out the omelette onto an oiled plate, then put the pan upside down over the plate and quickly invert the two. Gently pour the last measure of oil down the sides of the pan and under the omelette. Cook over high heat until firm and golden – about 5 minutes. Remove from the heat and slide the tortilla onto a serving plate.

Cool a little, then cut into cubes or wedges and eat while still warm.

Antipasti doesn't have to be full-on Italian. This kind of fresh, easy-to-assemble first course is a favourite in my native New Zealand, where the ingredients aren't always Mediterranean, but can incorporate the fresh Asian flavours so popular there. Don't be afraid to create your own combinations.

# modern antipasti platter

Prepare either a large serving platter or 4 separate plates and arrange a row of mozzarella or goats' cheese, caperberries or capers, fennel, and prawns or crayfish. Add a second row of nuts or olives, prosciutto and figs. Arrange each one in small piles, twists or stacks.

Put the tomatoes, still on their vines, onto an oiled baking tray and roast in a preheated oven at 220°C (425°F) Gas 7 for 8–10 minutes or until blistered, soft, dark and aromatic. Add to the second row on the platter or plates.

Put the fish sauce or soy sauce into a bowl, add half the oil and half the mint, then mash together. Trickle the mixture over the cheese, caperberries, fennel and prawns or crayfish, then sprinkle with the remaining herbs, then the sesame seeds.

Use the remaining oil to sprinkle over the nuts or olives, prosciutto, figs and tomatoes. Serve cool within 30 minutes.

YOUR CHOICE OF:

**125 g mozzarella or mild goats' cheese, sliced or torn**

**4 tablespoons caperberries or capers, rinsed**

**1 fennel bulb, finely sliced lengthways**

**4 cooked king prawns or crayfish tails, in the shell**

**4 tablespoons salted macadamia nuts, pistachio nuts, or black olives**

**4 slices prosciutto**

**4 fresh figs, halved lengthways**

**4 bunches of cherry tomatoes, on the vine**

**leaves from a small bunch of mint**

**2 teaspoons fish sauce or soy sauce**

**125 ml extra virgin olive oil**

**1 tablespoon toasted sesame seeds**

**SERVES 4**

Tiny, delicious, bite-sized fish cakes make perfect, easy finger foods. They are an essential taste of Thailand, yet have now travelled all over Europe and America. Use whatever fish you like – white fish, salmon or trout are all good.

# spicy thai fish cakes

**1 kg fish, such as salmon or trout, skinned, boned and cubed**

**8 shallots or small red onions**

**5 cm fresh ginger, finely chopped (optional)**

**1 stalk of lemongrass, finely sliced**

**a large bunch of coriander, chopped**

**4 garlic cloves, chopped**

**4 kaffir lime leaves, sliced hair-thin**

**1 tablespoon caster sugar**

**1 tablespoon fish sauce or soy sauce**

**250 g thin asparagus, finely sliced**

**salt and freshly ground black pepper**

**peanut oil, for brushing**

**lime wedges or chilli sauce, to serve**

**MAKES 42: SERVES 6**

Put the fish, shallots or onions, ginger, lemongrass, coriander, garlic, lime leaves, sugar and fish sauce or soy sauce into a non-metal bowl and let marinate for 10 minutes to allow the flavours to develop. Transfer to a food processor and work to a coarse mince: do not reduce to a paste. Stir in the sliced asparagus, salt and pepper.

Shape the mixture into walnut-size balls, about 42, then flatten into cakes 1 cm thick. Season well. Heat a stove-top grill pan or frying pan and brush with oil. Add the fish cakes in batches and cook for 1–1½ minutes on each side, or until golden and cooked right through. Serve the fish cakes with lime wedges or a small bowl of chilli sauce.

Char-grilling, using spicy marinades, is a favourite Vietnamese cooking method. These brochettes are pungent and spicy-hot: not for the faint-hearted. At a pinch, lemons could stand in for limes, but limes epitomize fresh Vietnamese flavours better. Fresh herbs and salad leaves are also typical.

**750 g boneless chicken breasts or thighs**

**2 tablespoons black peppercorns**

**2 tablespoons Szechuan peppercorns or green peppercorns**

**1 tablespoon sea salt flakes**

**4 tablespoons apricot jam**

**4 garlic cloves, crushed**

**2 tablespoons fish sauce**

**shredded zest and freshly squeezed juice of 2 limes**

TO SERVE (OPTIONAL)

**2 Little Gem or baby cos lettuces, leaves separated**

**2 small bundles of beanthread noodles, 30 g each, soaked in just-boiled water for about 3 minutes**

**5 cm cucumber, sliced and diced**

**a handful of mint sprigs**

*12 wooden satay sticks, soaked in water for 30 minutes*

**SERVES 4**

Beat the chicken pieces flat using a meat mallet or the flat side of a Chinese cleaver: this will also tenderize them. Cut into 2.5 cm cubes, about 48.

Put the peppercorns into a dry frying pan and toast over medium heat, shaking constantly until aromatic but not scorched. Transfer to an electric spice grinder and grind until coarse and gritty. Alternatively, use a mortar and pestle. Transfer to a shallow non-metal dish, add the salt, jam, garlic, fish sauce and lime juice. Reserve some of the lime zest for serving and add the remainder to the dish. Mix to a sticky paste.

Add the chicken pieces to the paste and stir until well coated. Push the chicken, 4 cubes at a time, onto the soaked satay sticks.

Preheat a grill or barbecue. Set the chicken skewers about 7.5 cm from the heat and cook for 4–5 minutes on each side. Serve with a platter of lettuce leaves, noodles, cucumber and mint.

To eat, remove the chicken from the skewers, fill lettuce leaves with noodles and cucumber, add the chicken, then top with mint and the reserved lime zest.

# vietnamese peppery chicken

# miniature spring rolls

Spring rolls should be lean, crisp and refreshing and make effortless party snacks. Serve them with your favourite dipping sauces – I like grated ginger in a little sweetened rice vinegar. Keep the spring roll wrappers covered with plastic while you work, so they don't dry out.

Blanch the beansprouts for 1 minute in boiling water, then refresh in iced water. Top and tail them, discarding the ends. Put into a bowl, add the other vegetables and the ginger and mix gently.

Heat the 3 tablespoons oil, add the vegetables and stir-fry for 1–1½ minutes. Add the beancurd, sugar, soy sauce and rice wine or sherry, then cook for 1 minute longer. Let cool, then divide into 8 portions (each will be enough for 4–5 spring rolls).

Cut each wrapper in half diagonally. Put 1 portion of filling onto the long side, a third of the way from the edge. Fold the long side over the filling, then fold over the side flaps. Roll up. Mix the flour and water and dab a little of the mixture on the pointed end of the roll. Press to seal. Set the rolls on a lightly floured surface, not touching, until all are made.

Heat the oil to 190°C (375°F) or a little hotter, but do not let it smoke. Deep-fry the rolls, 8–10 at a time, for 3–4 minutes. Remove with a wire strainer, drain on crumpled kitchen paper and keep hot in a low oven. Let the oil reheat before cooking the next batch.

When all the spring rolls have been cooked, serve with your choice of dips, such as chilli sauce, soy sauce, or grated ginger mixed with equal quantities of rice vinegar, sesame oil and honey.

**125 g fresh beansprouts**

**75 g spring onions, finely sliced**

**75 g carrots, finely sliced**

**75 g bamboo shoots, fresh or soaked, finely sliced**

**75 g fresh shiitake mushrooms, stems discarded, caps finely sliced**

**5 cm fresh ginger, finely sliced**

**3 tablespoons peanut oil, plus extra, for frying**

**50 g firm beancurd (tofu), finely diced**

**2 teaspoons caster sugar**

**1 tablespoon light soy sauce**

**1 tablespoon Chinese rice wine or dry sherry**

**20 spring roll wrappers or wonton skins**

**2 tablespoons flour**

**2 tablespoons water**

**MAKES 36–40: SERVES 6–8**

Put the chicken, pepper and vodka or gin into a bowl, stir well, cover and set aside while you prepare the other ingredients.

Put the egg white into a second bowl and whisk to a froth. Beat in the bacon or cream, then the sesame oil, ginger, salt, garlic and parsley.

Slowly beat in the chicken mixture, spring onions and water chestnuts until evenly combined, but do not overmix. Alternatively, gently knead it together using your hands (the authentic method).

Using kitchen scissors or a large biscuit cutter, cut a round as large as possible from each square wonton wrapper. Put 1 tablespoon of the filling onto each one. Using a small spatula, smooth the mixture almost to the edges.

Put the filled wonton into the palm of one hand and cup your fingers around it, pushing the mixture down with the spatula – you will achieve an open, pleated purse shape. Drop it gently onto a floured work surface to flatten the bottom and settle the filling.

Arrange the dumplings, without letting them touch each other, in a bamboo steamer or steamers. Heat a wok or saucepan of boiling water on top of the stove, set the steamer on top and steam, covered, for about 7–10 minutes, refilling the base with boiling water as necessary. Serve hot, topped with coriander or chives, accompanied by your choice of sauces or dips.

**500 g chicken breast, diced then minced**

**1 teaspoon freshly ground white pepper**

**2 tablespoons vodka or gin**

**1 egg white**

**3 slices smoked streaky bacon or 4 tablespoons cream**

**2 teaspoons sesame oil**

**2 teaspoons grated fresh ginger**

**2 teaspoons sea salt flakes**

**2 teaspoons crushed garlic**

**2 tablespoons finely chopped parsley**

**4 spring onions, green and white, finely chopped**

**4 water chestnuts, canned or fresh and peeled, finely diced**

**30–45 square wonton wrappers**

**sprigs of coriander or chives, to serve**

**MAKES 30–45: SERVES 4–6**

# steamed moneybags

These little Chinese dumplings are incredibly easy to make. Cook them in layers in a bamboo steamer and serve them straight from the steamer as party food. You can serve one layer while the next one cooks.

# baby pizzas

There's nothing better than homemade pizza (once you've tried it, you'll never bother with ready-made again). They are incredibly easy to make – all you need is a food processor. Make them large – or small like these, so everyone can taste a different topping.

**500 g unbleached plain flour**

**2 sachets easy-blend dried yeast, 7 g each**

**1 teaspoon salt**

**4 tablespoons extra virgin olive oil**

TOPPINGS

**250 ml fresh tomato sauce, tapenade or sun-dried tomato pesto**

**250 ml sautéed spinach, rocket or roasted peppers**

**100 g black olives and/or capers**

**50 g anchovies, halved lengthways and/or toasted pine nuts**

**8 garlic cloves, chopped**

**1–2 tablespoons chopped fresh rosemary, sage or thyme**

**250 g mozzarella cheese, drained and cubed**

**250 ml extra virgin olive oil**

**sea salt flakes and freshly ground black pepper**

*2 baking sheets, lightly oiled*
*a round biscuit cutter, 5–7.5 cm diameter*

**MAKES 32–40: SERVES 8**

To make the dough, put the flour, yeast and salt into a food processor. Pulse briefly to sift the dry ingredients. Add the olive oil and 360 ml lukewarm water. Process in short bursts for 15 seconds to form a soft mass, not a ball.

Turn out onto a floured work surface, then knead by hand for 2 minutes, slamming down the dough 2–3 times to help develop the gluten. Put the dough into a clean, oiled bowl. Turn it over once to coat with oil. Put the bowl of dough into a large plastic bag, seal and let rise until doubled in size, about 1½ hours.

Put the dough onto the work surface and punch it down with oiled hands. Cut in half. Pat and roll out each piece to a circle about 5 mm thick. Push dimples all over it with your fingers.

Using the biscuit cutter, cut out about 16 small discs. Set them on a baking sheet. Top each one with ½–1 teaspoon of sauce, tapenade or pesto. Add spinach, rocket or roasted peppers, then a choice of olives, capers, anchovies or pine nuts. Add garlic, herbs or cheese. Season to taste and sprinkle with olive oil. Repeat, using the second half of the dough on a second baking sheet.

Set aside for 15–20 minutes, then bake at 240°C (475°F) Gas 9 for 12–15 minutes or until the bases are blistered and crisp, the toppings aromatic and the cheese melted. Serve hot.

12 slices bread, such as light rye, pumpernickel or rye with caraway seeds, or a combination of all three

50 g unsalted butter

TROUT TOPPING

2 rainbow trout fillets, skinned

90 ml white wine vinegar

25 g sugar cubes

2 tablespoons sea salt flakes

1 red onion, finely sliced into rings

4 cornichons (baby gherkins), sliced

GRAVAD LAX TOPPING

250 g gravad lax or smoked salmon

freshly ground black pepper

6 sprigs of dill

PRAWN TOPPING

24 cooked prawns, shelled

chives or sprigs of flat leaf parsley

2 tablespoons homemade mayonnaise (page 43)

4 lemon wedges

**MAKES 12: SERVES 6**

Danish open sandwiches are like 'retro' bruschetta. All you need is good bread – a light rye is traditional. Spread it with a little butter so the topping doesn't make it soggy, then load it up with your favourite things. I've used some store-bought seafood toppings to save time, but try this homemade marinated trout as well – it's easy to do and tastes terrific.

# danish open sandwiches
## with three seafood toppings

To make the trout topping, start a little ahead. Put the fillets into a non-metal dish about 5 cm deep. Put the vinegar, sugar and salt into a saucepan, heat and stir to dissolve, then let cool slightly. Pour over the fillets, cover and chill for 1–2 hours.

Just before serving, butter the bread (this will seal the bread as well as helping the toppings to stick).

Set several slices of gravad lax or smoked salmon on each of 4 slices of bread. Add the pepper and a sprig of dill.

Drain the trout, pat dry with kitchen paper and slice into thin diagonal strips. Put several onto 4 slices of bread. Add the red onion rings and cornichons.

Pile 6 prawns each onto 4 slices of bread. Add chives or parsley, mayonnaise and a wedge of lemon.

Serve the prepared sandwiches on a board or large platter.

Two great Mediterranean ways with toasted bread – one from Italy and the other from Catalonia in Spain. The essential requirements are a good, rustic loaf and quality olive oil. The tomato and garlic are classic Catalonian, but bruschetta can be topped with whatever you fancy.

# bruschetta with mushrooms and cheese

**8 slices Italian country-style bread such as puglièse, cut 2.5 cm thick**

**4–6 garlic cloves, crushed but not peeled**

**6–8 tablespoons extra virgin olive oil**

**250 g mushrooms preserved in oil, such as porcini, drained and sliced**

**250 g Gorgonzola or dolcelatte cheese**

**sea salt and freshly ground black pepper**

**SERVES 4 OR 8**

Grill, char-grill, toast or barbecue the bread on both sides. While the bread is still hot, quickly rub the garlic directly over one surface, discarding the skin as the flesh wears down. Sprinkle with enough olive oil to soak into the hot, garlicky toasts. Arrange the mushroom slices over one half of each piece and add a smear of cheese over the other. Add salt (take care: blue cheeses can be very salty) and pepper. Serve immediately.

**Variations** Instead of the porcini, use smoked artichoke hearts preserved in oil, or top the toasts with 250 g cooked cannellini beans mashed with 2 cloves crushed garlic. Top with sautéed greens, such as rocket.

# pan amb tomaquet

Toast, grill, char-grill or barbecue the bread briefly on both sides, so it is crusty outside, soft inside. Rub one side of each slice with garlic. Cut the tomato in half and use the cut sides to rub all over the garlic side of each toast (your guests can also do it themselves).

Top the toasts with loosely gathered folds of jamon serrano, Parma ham or prosciutto. Sprinkle oil generously all over each one.

Finely chop the remaining tomato flesh into tiny bits and scatter them over the top. Serve while the toasts are still warm.

**4 large, thick slices country-style bread**

**2 garlic cloves, halved**

**1 large, very ripe tomato**

**6–8 slices thinly sliced jamon serrano, Parma ham or prosciutto**

**3–4 tablespoons extra virgin olive oil**

**sea salt**

**SERVES 4–6**

# tortilla wraps with fresh green salsa

Wraps are some of the easiest and most casual dishes to prepare. All you need is some warmed flour tortillas, then your choice of fillings. This recipe uses refried beans, cheese and salsa, but you can add char-grilled meats, roasted chicken and whatever else you love. Canned refried (twice-cooked) beans can be made even more thick and spicy if you mash in chopped garlic, then heat in a pan with extra oil, cumin, chilli, salt and oregano, so they're substantial, hot and packed with flavour.

8 corn or flour tortillas, 20 cm diameter

250 g canned hot refried beans

2 teaspoons chopped fresh jalapeño or serrano chilli

¼ crisp lettuce, such as iceberg, sliced

125 g mature Cheddar cheese, grated coarsely

100 g pitted olives, green or black

125 ml sour cream

8 cherry tomatoes, chopped (optional)

sprigs of coriander (optional)

2 fresh red chillies, chopped (optional)

FRESH GREEN SALSA

4 spring onions, chopped

a handful of mint leaves

a handful of coriander leaves

2 teaspoons sea salt flakes

8 whole allspice or black peppercorns, crushed

freshly squeezed juice of 1 lime

MAKES 8

To make the salsa, put the spring onions, mint, coriander, salt, crushed allspice or peppercorns and lime juice into a bowl. Mix gently, then chill and use within 2 days.

To soften the tortillas, spray them with a little water, wrap in foil and cook in a preheated oven at 180°C (350°F) Gas Mark 4 for about 10–12 minutes until warm and pliable. Alternatively, wrap in baking parchment and microwave on HIGH for 3–4 minutes, or wrap in foil and heat in a bamboo steamer over boiling water for 5–10 minutes.

Spread 2–3 tablespoons of the refried beans on each tortilla. Add the chilli, lettuce, cheese, olives, salsa and cream. Fold up the base of the tortilla, then fold over the 2 sides, like an envelope. Serve warm, with cherry tomatoes, coriander or red chillies, if using.

250 g quick-cook 'instant' polenta

olive oil, for brushing

6 slices Parma ham

a few salad leaves, such as rocket, watercress or frisée

freshly ground black pepper

25 g Parmesan cheese, shaved into long, thin slivers with a vegetable peeler

about 3 tablespoons extra virgin olive oil, or to taste

*a springform cake tin, 20–25 cm diameter, oiled*

**SERVES 6**

Cook the polenta, following the packet instructions, until thick and creamy. Spoon the mixture into the prepared cake tin and spread the top evenly with the back of a tablespoon. Let cool for 15–30 minutes or until dense and firmly set.

Cut into wedges. If the cake of polenta is very thick, cut it horizontally crossways first to make two discs, then slice into 6–12 segments like a cake.

Preheat a ridged, cast-iron, stove-top grill pan until very, very hot. Brush the polenta wedges with a little olive oil, then press them onto the pan and cook for about 8–15 minutes (you must heat it thoroughly as well as frizzling the crust). Using a fish slice or tongs, turn the pieces and cook the other side for the same length of time.

To serve, set 1 slice on each plate and drape a slice of prosciutto over and beside it. Add the salad leaves, sprinkle with pepper and shavings of Parmesan, then trickle over the extra virgin olive oil and serve immediately.

# char-grilled polenta with proscuitto

Making polenta used to be a rather time-consuming activity. These days, you can find quick-cook polenta, so it's much faster and easier. Cook according to the packet instructions, then pour into a springform cake tin, let cool and set. Remove from the tin, cut into wedges and char-grill on a stove-top grill pan. Great with traditional Italian prosciutto.

My mother-in-law, Joyce, taught me the recipe for this simple, semi-smooth pâté. The whole thing can be made in less than 10 minutes. It can be eaten warm, but is usually better cooled and chilled (I use the freezer for speed). Wonderful as a first course, or for parties, and a thousand times better than any of the store-bought pâtés.

# chicken liver pâté

Put one-third of the butter into a non-stick frying pan and heat gently. Add the livers and sauté over high heat for 2 minutes, stirring constantly. Standing well back from the pan, carefully add the brandy and light it with a match. Let flame for 1–2 minutes, shaking the pan, then add the garlic, onion, salt and nutmeg and cook for a further 2 minutes until the liquid has almost all evaporated and the livers and onion are golden. (Ideally, the livers should still be pink inside.)

Add the thyme and another one-third of the butter and heat until the butter has melted.

Transfer the mixture to a food processor. Blend, in 4–5 short bursts, to a semi-smooth paste. Spoon into 1 large or 4 small china pots. Smooth the surface. Melt the remaining butter. Pour it over the surface, adding a decorative topping of thyme and peppercorns, pushing them into the butter.

Let cool, then put into the freezer for at least 1 hour. Transfer to the refrigerator and chill for 1–2 hours until very cold and firm. Serve the same day with Melba toast or crisp, toasted slices of baguette, or store longer: the flavours improve for up to a week.

**150 g salted butter, cubed**

**250 g chicken livers, trimmed and halved**

**4 tablespoons brandy**

**2 garlic cloves, crushed**

**1 onion, chopped**

**½ teaspoon sea salt flakes**

**¼ teaspoon freshly grated nutmeg**

**2–3 tablespoons fresh thyme leaves**

TO SERVE

**sprigs of thyme**

**about 20 peppercorns**

**SERVES 6–8**

# sauces

& dips

# vinaigrette

Fresh vinaigrette is so easy to make, I don't know why anyone ever buys it ready-made. Just put into a jar and shake, or into a salad bowl and beat briefly with a fork.

**75 ml white or red wine vinegar (1 part)**
**225–375 ml extra virgin olive oil (3–5 parts)**
**sea salt and freshly ground white pepper**

**MAKES 300–450 ML**

Put all the ingredients into a bowl, vinaigrette flask or screwtop jar. Whisk, beat or shake to form a temporary emulsion. Store in a cool, dark place (the oil can become rancid in bright sunlight and heat). Use within 1 week – and shake again before serving.

To make a smaller amount – enough for one salad – use 1 part vinegar to 3–5 parts oil, plus seasoning to taste. If preferred, pour the ingredients into the salad bowl and beat them with a fork. Put the salad on top and leave undisturbed – no longer than 30 minutes – then toss just before serving.

# mayonnaise

Making real mayonnaise with a hand-held electric mixer is blissfully quick and easy – just 5 minutes. It turns any salad into a feast.

Put the yolks into a medium bowl with high, straight sides and a curved base. Stir in the mustard, salt and half the lemon juice or vinegar, then beat until smooth. Mix the oils in a small jug, then, with the oil jug in one hand and a hand-held electric mixer in the other, gradually pour in the oil, whisking continuously, to form a stiff, glossy emulsion. When all the oil has been added, taste, then whisk or beat in the remaining juice or vinegar. Taste and adjust the seasoning. Cover the surface with clingfilm until ready to use. Best used immediately, it may be also refrigerated for up to 3 days.

**2 egg yolks, at room temperature**

**2 teaspoons Dijon mustard**

**¼ teaspoon salt**

**2 teaspoons fresh lemon juice or white wine vinegar**

**200 ml extra virgin olive oil**

**175 m mild oil, such as grapeseed, safflower or sunflower oil**

**MAKES 400 ML**

# pesto

Make your own pesto in the height of summer, when there are big, strong bunches of basil in the market. Homemade, it's a revelation.

Put the pine nuts into a small frying pan, add 1 teaspoon of the olive oil and stir-fry quickly until golden. Remove and let cool.

Put the pine nuts, garlic, salt and basil into a food processor and work to a paste. Alternatively, use a mortar and pestle.

With the machine still running, add half the cheese, then gradually pour in half the remaining olive oil. Add the remaining cheese and oil all at once and work or blend again. The paste should be a vivid green.

**100 g pine nuts**

**125 ml extra virgin olive oil**

**6 garlic cloves, chopped**

**1 teaspoon coarse sea salt or rock salt**

**25 g fresh basil leaves, torn**

**50 g freshly grated Parmesan cheese**

**50 g freshly grated pecorino cheese**

**MAKES ABOUT 250 ML**

# tsatziki yoghurt sauce

Yoghurt in Greece is so rich, sharp and solid that it's almost like cheese, not yoghurt. If you can't find the real thing, strain plain yoghurt through a muslin-lined sieve or mash it with cream cheese or even feta cheese for stiffness.

Grate the cucumber coarsely, put into a non-metal bowl, sprinkle with the salt, stir and let stand for 5 minutes. Put into a non-metal sieve and press hard to squeeze out the salt and liquid. Do not rinse. Return to a clean bowl and stir in the garlic and yoghurt. Spoon into small individual serving dishes and sprinkle with a little olive oil. Serve with chopped herbs, black olives, bread, cucumber and carrot.

**250 g cucumber, unpeeled**

**2 teaspoons salt**

**3 garlic cloves, crushed**

**375 ml strained plain Greek yoghurt**

**4 tablespoons extra virgin olive oil**

TO SERVE (OPTIONAL)

**fresh mint or parsley, chopped**

**black olives and bread**

**cucumber, cut into strips**

**carrots, cut into strips**

**MAKES ABOUT 700 ML: SERVES 4–6**

# harissa paste

Harissa paste is an exciting, incendiary condiment. It is sold in cans or jars, but is easy to make yourself.

An hour before making the sauce, reserve 3 of the dried chillies, then carefully discard all the seeds and membranes from the remainder. Put all the chillies into a bowl and cover with about 500 ml boiling water. Set aside until rehydrated, about 30 minutes.

Drain the plumped-up chillies (reserving 2 tablespoons of the soaking liquid) and scissor-chop them directly into a blender (wear rubber gloves if you are sensitive to chillies). Chop the roasted red peppers and add to the blender with the garlic, salt, cumin, coriander and paprika.

Add the reserved 2 tablespoons of soaking liquid, plus most of the olive oil, 5–6 tablespoons. Blend to a smooth, red, creamy sauce. Refrigerate and use within 2 weeks or freeze for up to 1 month.

Use for enlivening couscous or pasta, in vinaigrette or mayonnaise, or stirred through tagines.

**30 g large, dried, hot chillies such as cascabel or Kashmiri**

**2 large red peppers, char-grilled or roasted, then skinned and deseeded**

**4 garlic cloves, crushed**

**½–1 teaspoon salt**

**2 tablespoons cumin seeds, coarsely crushed**

**2 tablespoons coriander seeds, coarsely crushed**

**2 tablespoons mild paprika**

**125 ml extra virgin olive oil**

**MAKES 300 ML**

# hoummus

Lemony, fresh hoummus is a delicious Middle Eastern snack. For 10-minute hoummus, use canned chickpeas, but cook dried chickpeas, if you have time.

200 g dried chickpeas or 400 g cooked or canned

freshly squeezed juice of 1 lemon

2 garlic cloves, crushed

¼ teaspoon salt

freshly ground black pepper

2 tablespoons tahini paste (optional)

125 ml first-pressing extra virgin olive oil

TO SERVE

hot paprika and extra virgin olive oil

MAKES 400 ML: SERVES 6–8:

If using dried chickpeas, put them into a bowl and cover with boiling water for 3 hours. Drain. Put into a large saucepan, cover with boiling water, bring to the boil and simmer for 1½–2½ hours or until the chickpeas are easily crushable and tender. Drain.

Put the cooked or canned chickpeas into a food processor, add the lemon juice, garlic, salt, pepper and the tahini paste, if using. Blend briefly to a mousse. With the machine running, gently pour the oil through the feed tube to form a creamy purée. Season to taste.

Serve cool or chilled, sprinkled with a little hot red paprika and extra virgin olive oil.

# taramasalata

Real, homemade taramasalata is a revelation – quite different from the lurid, tasteless, manufactured variety. Specialist delicatessens sell authentic smoked or salted cod's roe.

Put the cod's roe, bread and lemon juice into a food processor. Purée in brief bursts. With the machine running, slowly pour in the oil, very slowly, through the feed tube, to form a pale, dense emulsion. With the machine still running, very gradually drizzle in 3–4 tablespoons boiling water to lighten the mixture. Stir in the onions. Serve with black olives, raw fennel or crisp celery and warmed pita breads.

**Note** If making with a mortar and pestle, omit the bread. You can also add crushed garlic at the end: not traditional, but delicious.

2 tablespoons pressed salted cod's roe, uncoloured, or 110 g smoked cod's roe

50 g stale bread, wetted, squeezed dry, then crumbled

freshly squeezed juice of ½ lemon

250 ml extra virgin olive oil

4 tablespoons chopped red onion, blanched in boiling water for 1 minute

1 large garlic clove, crushed (optional)

**SERVES 6–8: MAKES 400 ML**

# skordalia walnut sauce

Skordalia is a favourite Greek sauce – serve it with poultry, pork, smoked fish or with crisp raw vegetables. It's also good as a dip or spread.

**50 g stale country bread, cubed**

**1 tablespoon wine vinegar**

**50 g walnut halves, coarsely chopped**

**½–1 teaspoon salt**

**2–3 garlic cloves, crushed**

**6 tablespoons extra virgin olive oil**

**125 ml thick Greek yoghurt**

**MAKES 300 ML: SERVES 4**

Put the bread into a sieve and set it over a bowl. Pour over hot water, then drain the bread and press it down to squeeze dry. Crumble it into a food processor. Add the vinegar, walnuts, salt and garlic, then pulse in brief bursts to a thick, coarse paste. Slowly pour in 4 tablespoons of the oil and process until creamy. Fold in the yoghurt to give a slightly marbled effect. Pile into a bowl. Sprinkle with the remaining olive oil and serve cool.

# tapenade

This delicious, intense black olive paste is good as a dip or spread for bread, but can also be used as a sauce for fish, or folded through other sauces, purées or pasta to give a Mediterranean flavour.

**350 g salt-cured black olives, pitted (250 g after pitting)**

**50 g canned anchovies**

**100 g canned tuna in olive oil, drained**

**3 garlic cloves, crushed**

**½ teaspoon dried oregano or marjoram**

**50 g pickled or salted capers, rinsed and drained**

**60 ml extra virgin olive oil**

**2 tablespoons brandy**

**sea salt and freshly ground black pepper**

**MAKES 500 ML: SERVES 4–6**

Put the pitted olives, anchovies, tuna, garlic, oregano or marjoram, capers, salt and pepper into a food processor. Alternatively, use a mortar and pestle. Work to a messy paste, then slowly pour the oil through the feed tube, in pulsing bursts. Taste and adjust the seasoning. Pour in half the brandy and purée again.

Spoon the mixture into a bowl and sprinkle the remaining brandy over the top. Serve with crusty bread, garlicky bread, crostini, breadsticks, crisp raw vegetables or baked seafood.

**Note** Don't even consider using the pre-pitted, unripe, dyed black olives sometimes available from the USA. Proper tree-ripened black olives, pitted at home, are essential.

# salads &

# vegetables

2 handfuls of peppery leaves,
such as rocket or watercress

2 handfuls of bitter leaves, such as frisée

2 handfuls of crisp green lettuce,
such as Little Gem or cos, torn

1 small head of chicory (witloof), separated into leaves

1 small head of baby spinach leaves

leaves from a small bunch of flat leaf parsley,
dill or mint (optional)

1 small onion, finely sliced into rings

DRESSING

2 garlic cloves, crushed

½ teaspoon sea salt flakes

1–1½ tablespoons freshly squeezed lemon juice
or cider vinegar

4–6 tablespoons extra virgin olive oil

**SERVES 4**

To make the dressing, put the garlic, salt and half the lemon juice into a small bowl and mix with a hand-held stick blender or a fork. Slowly pour in the oil and blend or mix until a rich emulsion forms. Taste, then add enough lemon juice to give bite. Alternatively, use a mortar and pestle.

Put the washed leaves, herbs, if using, and onion rings into a large bowl, cover with a plastic bag, seal and chill until ready to serve, so the leaves stay crisp and fresh.

Just before serving, trickle the dressing over the leaves and toss thoroughly with your hands or 2 wooden spoons.

# fresh green salad

A green salad is the easiest of dishes to assemble, but, to be successful, the ingredients must be very good quality. Choose a selection of leaves (soft and crisp, sweet and bitter), then dress with best extra virgin olive oil, the lightest touch of vinegar or lemon juice and just the right amount of seasoning.

The trick with oranges is to remove all the bitter white pith. Cut a slice off the top and bottom of the fruit, stand it on the base, then slice off the peel from top to bottom. Keep all the juice to add to the dressing.

# moroccan orange salad
## with olives and onions

**4–6 large oranges, about 675 g**

**1 teaspoon harissa paste (page 44)**

**4 tablespoons extra virgin olive oil**

**2 red onions, finely sliced into rings**

**about 20 green olives stuffed with anchovies**

**about 20 dry-cured black olives**

**sprigs of mint, to serve**

**SERVES 4–6**

Wash and dry the oranges and, using a zester or grater, remove about 1 tablespoon of zest shreds and set aside. Using a sharp knife, remove and discard the skin, pith and the outer membranes.

Slice the oranges crossways, reserving all the juices. Put the collected juices, harissa paste and olive oil into a bowl and whisk to form a pinky-red dressing. (If there doesn't seem to be enough juice, squeeze one of the orange slices and add its juices as well.) Put the sliced onions into a bowl, cover with boiling water, leave for 2 minutes, then drain. Plunge into a bowl of iced water to refresh and cool, then drain again.

Arrange the sliced oranges on a platter. Add the onion rings and olives, trickle the dressing over the top, then add the orange zest and sprigs of mint. Serve cool.

An outrageously easy salad – but, as always, best quality ingredients are essential. Buy very ripe, red tomatoes, extra virgin olive oil and good mozzarella – buffalo is best.

# mozzarella and tomato salad
## with wild rocket and olives

**3 mozzarella cheeses, 150 g each**

**4 large, juicy, sun-ripened red tomatoes**

**4 large handfuls of fresh wild rocket, about 350 g**

**6–8 tablespoons extra virgin olive oil**

**sea salt and freshly ground black pepper**

**black olives, to serve (optional)**

**SERVES 4**

Drain the mozzarella cheeses. Slice thickly or pull them apart into big rough chunks, showing the grainy strands. Arrange down one side of a large serving platter.

Cut the tomatoes into thick slices and arrange them in a second line down the middle of the plate. If they are very large, cut them in half first, then into semi-circles. Add the rocket leaves on the other side of the platter.

Sprinkle with salt and pepper, then trickle the olive oil over the top just before serving. Serve with crusty bread (slightly char-grilled tastes good) to mop up the juices and add the black olives, if using.

Chorizo – Spanish salami – adds extra pizzazz to many dishes. I like to fry it first to release all the smoky paprika juices. Nothing could be simpler or have more impact. It's available from many supermarkets and most good delicatessens.

# warm chicken and chorizo salad

Heat a non-stick frying pan or stove-top grill pan, add the chorizo slices or chunks, then fry gently on all sides until the juices run and the edges are slightly crisp. Set aside.

Put the vinaigrette ingredients into a small bowl or jug and mix well. Use some of the mixture to brush the courgette halves, then add them to the still-hot pan and cook for 5 minutes on each side or until hot and golden.

Put the chicken into a large salad bowl and add the lettuce leaves and olives. Sprinkle with the remaining vinaigrette, then add the courgette, the chorizo and its juices and the parsley or coriander. Toss well, then serve immediately with garlic bread, toasted ciabatta or warmed focaccia.

3 mild or spicy chorizo sausages, about 100 g, cut crossways into coin-shaped slices, or a 150 g piece, cut into chunks

12–16 baby courgettes, about 300 g, halved lengthways

500 g boneless, skinless, cooked or smoked chicken, shredded into strips

250 g mixed red and green lettuce leaves

1 bag rocket or watercress, about 100 g

16–20 dry-cured black olives, about 75 g

sprigs of coriander or flat leaf parsley

VINAIGRETTE

2 tablespoons balsamic vinegar

6 tablespoons extra virgin olive oil

2 garlic cloves, crushed

sea salt and freshly ground black pepper

SERVES 4

# spanish roasted vegetable salad

Serve this easy dish hot, warm or cool, and with lots of good, crusty, country bread to mop up the juices.

**2 red peppers**

**2 yellow peppers**

**½ butternut squash or 500 g pumpkin, unpeeled**

**2 red onions, unpeeled**

**2 Spanish onions, unpeeled**

**6–8 medium vine-ripened tomatoes**

**125 ml extra virgin olive oil, preferably Spanish**

**sea salt and freshly ground black pepper**

**SERVES 4–6**

Cut the peppers in half lengthways, slicing through the stems. Leave these intact, but discard the pith and seeds.

Slice the butternut squash or pumpkin, into 2.5 cm discs or chunks.

Cut the onions crossways into halves, leaving the roots and tops intact. Leave the skins on, too – they give extra colour and flavour and protect the shape.

Put all the vegetables, including the tomatoes, cut sides up, into a large, lightly oiled roasting tin. Sprinkle half the oil over the vegetables and season with sea salt and pepper.

Roast towards the top of a preheated oven at 240°C (475°F) Gas 9 for 30 minutes, until the vegetables are frizzled, fragrant, wrinkled and soft.

Sprinkle the remaining oil over the top and serve hot, warm or cool. Eat the salad with your fingers, discarding the skins, roots and stems along the way.

**Note** Use bread to scoop up the sweet, oily, sticky juices from the hot tin – superb.

# vermicelli noodle salad
## with duck breast

Dried noodles are a great standby. Some, like beanthread noodles (also known as cellophane or glass noodles), don't even have to be cooked – just soaked in hot water until softened. Rice flour noodles like these should be soaked first, then cooked for only about a minute. Wheat or buckwheat noodles, made with or without eggs, have to be cooked the longest, but even then only for about 5–6 minutes at the most.

250 g dried rice stick vermicelli noodles

3 tablespoons corn oil

4 shallots, chopped

2.5 cm fresh ginger, finely sliced lengthways

350 g smoked duck breast, sliced

8–12 fresh shiitake mushrooms, stems discarded, caps sliced

1 small head of spring cabbage, bok choy or Chinese leaves, finely sliced

4 spring onions, sliced lengthways

1 tablespoon light soy sauce

250 ml chicken stock

1 teaspoon sugar

1 teaspoon salt

1 tablespoon chopped fresh parsley

1 tablespoon chopped fresh chives or Chinese chives

1 tablespoon chopped fresh coriander

SERVES 4

Put the noodles into a bowl, then cover with hot water for about 6–8 minutes (any longer and they will soften too much). Drain just before using and, while still warm, scissor-cut into half lengths to make handling easier.

Working quickly, heat the oil in a wok, add the shallots and ginger, then stir-fry briskly for 2 minutes. Add the smoked duck and mushrooms and cook, covered, for 1 minute.

Add the cabbage, bok choy or Chinese leaves, spring onions and warm noodles. Add the soy sauce, chicken stock, sugar and salt. Cook until the liquid has been absorbed – about 2–3 minutes. Serve hot, warm or cold, sprinkled with the herbs.

Aubergines cook surprisingly quickly, especially when cut into slices and grilled or fried. Cook right through: aubergines don't taste good if undercooked, so make sure they have become translucent, with no trace of white.

# aubergine antipasto
## with pine nuts and herbs

**2–3 medium aubergines, about 700 g**

**2 tablespoons sea salt flakes**

**about 125 ml extra virgin olive oil**

**50 g pine nuts**

**a small bunch of fresh mint, half chopped, half in sprigs**

**a small bunch of fresh flat leaf parsley, half chopped, half in sprigs**

**a few drops of aged balsamic vinegar**

**sea salt and freshly ground black pepper**

**SERVES 4–6**

Slice the aubergines lengthways into 1 cm slices. Score both sides of each slice with a fork. Sprinkle with salt. Drain on a rack for 10–20 minutes, then pat dry with kitchen paper.

Meanwhile, heat a ridged stove-top grill pan until very hot. Wipe with olive oil using a wad of crumpled kitchen paper or a heatproof brush. Paint each slice of aubergine with olive oil. Arrange on the hot pan, pressing down firmly. Cook for 3–5 minutes on each side until grill-marked, tender and aromatic. Heat 1 tablespoon olive oil in a frying pan, add the pine nuts and toast gently until golden. Set aside.

Scatter the cooked aubergine with chopped mint, chopped parsley, black pepper and a few drops of balsamic vinegar. Loop the slices on serving plates, add the pine nuts and sprigs of mint and parsley and serve as an antipasto.

**Note** If you grow your own aubergines and/or know they are the modern, hot-house-raised, non-bitter type, omit the salting process and continue with the recipe.

Stir-fried vegetables must be one of the easiest dishes ever. The only secret is to have all the ingredients prepared and assembled before you start cooking. The whole process is so fast that you won't have time to prepare anything in the middle of cooking the dish.

# stir-fried greens
## with cashew nuts

Drain the shiitakes, reserving some of the soaking liquid. Remove and discard their hard stems, cut the caps into halves or quarters, depending on size, and squeeze them dry.

Heat the oil in a wok or frying pan and stir-fry the cashew nuts, tossing and stirring until dark and crisp. Remove with a slotted spoon and set aside.

Add the bok choy and shiitakes and stir-fry, moving them rapidly around the wok, until crisp and tender. Add the salt, sugar, soy sauce, oyster or hoisin sauce and sesame oil. Add the cashew nuts, stir in about 2 tablespoons mushroom-soaking water and serve very hot while the nuts are still crisp.

**4 dried shiitake mushrooms, soaked in hand-hot water for 20 minutes**

**3 tablespoons peanut or soy oil**

**50 g cashew nuts**

**8–12 baby bok choy, halved lengthways**

**1 teaspoon salt**

**1 teaspoon sugar**

**1 tablespoon dark soy sauce**

**1 tablespoon oyster or hoisin sauce**

**1 tablespoon sesame oil**

**SERVES 4**

# catalan spinach
## with garlic, pine nuts and raisins

**2 tablespoons extra virgin olive oil, preferably Spanish**

**3 tablespoons pine nuts**

**2 garlic cloves, crushed**

**6 canned anchovy fillets, chopped**

**500 g well-washed spinach, water still clinging**

**3 tablespoons seedless raisins**

**salt and cracked black pepper**

**SERVES 3–4**

This easy, delicious dish can be used in lots of ways – piled on top of pizza, as a starter, or as an accompaniment to a main course.

Heat the oil in a non-stick frying pan. Carefully add the pine nuts, stir-fry for about 1 minute until golden, then remove quickly with a slotted spoon or drain through a sieve, reserving the oil and returning it to the pan.

Add the garlic and anchovies to the pan and mash them together over a medium heat until aromatic, then add the wet spinach and raisins. Toss carefully with non-stick tongs or wooden spoons until evenly distributed. Cover the pan and cook over medium heat for 2–3 minutes, stirring halfway through. Uncover the pan, sprinkle with the pine nuts and toss well until gleaming. Serve hot or warm, with small dishes of salt and cracked black pepper.

It can be served with garlicky toasts, sprinkled with olive oil or in warmed crusty rolls with slivers of cheese. This is also wonderful as a pizza topping, stirred into pasta or mixed into rice or couscous.

# tomatoes and peppers
## stuffed with rice and spices

Stuffed vegetables, such as peppers, mushrooms and tomatoes, are an easy classic. Leave out the lamb, change the chicken stock to vegetable stock, and the dish becomes a favourite with vegetarians, too.

Scoop the tomato pulp and seeds into a blender and pulse until well blended. Halve the peppers and remove and discard the seeds and membranes. Put the vegetable halves into a roasting tin and roast a preheated oven at 200°C (400°F) Gas Mark 6 for 10 minutes.

Meanwhile, heat the ghee or butter in a heavy-based frying pan. Add the garlic, onions, minced lamb, cinnamon sticks, turmeric, cumin, pepper and paprika and sauté for 5–6 minutes over high heat, stirring regularly.

Add the blended tomato pulp and seeds to the pan, then add the dried cranberries, rice, bulgar wheat and 600 ml of the stock. Season with salt. Add the mint and return to the boil, cover, then simmer for 10 minutes.

Spoon the mixture into the vegetable shells and spoon 1 tablespoon of reserved stock over each. Set the sliced tops back on top of the tomatoes. Cover the dish with a double layer of foil and return to the oven. Reduce the oven heat to 180°C (350°F) Gas Mark 5 and cook for about 40–45 minutes or until the rice is plumped up, all liquid is absorbed and the vegetables smell sweetly aromatic.

Top with the mint and a spoonful of yoghurt and serve with flatbreads.

4 large beefsteak tomatoes, tops sliced off and reserved

4 large peppers, with stems

2 tablespoons ghee or clarified butter

2 garlic cloves, chopped

2 onions, chopped

250 g finely minced lamb

2 cinnamon sticks, crushed

1 teaspoon ground turmeric

1 teaspoon cumin seeds, crushed

1 teaspoon cracked black pepper

1 teaspoon paprika

50 g dried cranberries

100 g basmati or other long grain rice

100 g bulgar wheat

750 ml chicken stock

½ teaspoon salt

2 teaspoons dried mint or
2 tablespoons sliced fresh mint

TO SERVE (OPTIONAL)

8 sprigs of mint

250 g plain yoghurt

pita or other Middle Eastern flatbreads

SERVES 4

Simple but superb – char-grilled corn, bathed in a fiery Mexican sauce. The cobs can be cooked on a stove-top grill pan or barbecue, under the grill or even roasted in the oven.

# char-grilled corn
## with Mexican red salsa

**8 ears of corn, with husks and silks**

**corn oil, for brushing**

**50 g diced unsalted butter (optional)**

RED SALSA

**2 slices of pineapple, fresh or canned**

**2 large plum tomatoes, halved lengthways**

**2 red peppers, halved lengthways**

**2 tablespoons olive oil**

**2 tablespoons brown sugar**

**2 dried chillies, preferably chipotles**

**1 teaspoon hot paprika**

**a small bunch of mint**

**6 tablespoons orange juice**

**½ teaspoon salt**

**SERVES 4 OR 8**

Heat a grill, stove-top grill pan or barbecue until very hot. Pull back the husks from the corn, remove the silks and rub or brush the kernels with oil. Grill or barbecue for 4–5 minutes on all sides or until brown, tender and fragrant. Alternatively, roast in a preheated oven at 200°C (400°F) Gas Mark 6 for 20–25 minutes.

Meanwhile, to make the Red Salsa, put the pineapple, tomatoes and peppers onto a baking sheet, brush with half the oil and sprinkle with sugar. Cook under a preheated grill for 6–8 minutes until slightly charred. Remove and discard the seeds and skins from the tomatoes and peppers (optional). Transfer the flesh to a food processor.

Put the remaining oil into a frying pan, heat gently, then add the chillies and cook for about 2–3 seconds on each side. Stem, chop and add to the food processor. Add the paprika, mint, juice and salt and blend to a coarse salsa. Alternatively, use a mortar and pestle.

**Variation** An even easier method is to roast the corn in a preheated oven at 200°C (400°F) Gas 6 for 18 minutes, add the pineapple, tomatoes and peppers and roast for another 8 minutes, then add the chillies and roast for 1 minute. Remove from the oven and proceed as in the main recipe.

# rice, pasta

# & noodles

Fragrant risotto, cooked until creamy, soupy, but with *al dente* bite, is comfort food of huge, timeless appeal. For ease, rice should be measured by volume, not weight. Keep the stock hot over gentle heat – this is the key to effortless success.

# porcini risotto
## with fresh and wild mushrooms

**15 g dried porcini mushrooms**

**50 g butter**

**100 g portobello or other large open mushrooms, quartered, or chanterelles, halved**

**6 tablespoons extra virgin olive oil**

**250 ml measured arborio rice**

**1 onion, sliced**

**2 garlic cloves, sliced**

**125 ml white wine**

**1 litre boiling chicken or veal stock**

**8 tablespoons freshly grated Parmesan cheese, about 50 g, plus extra shavings, to serve**

**sea salt**

**SERVES 4**

Put the dried porcini into a small bowl, add 250 ml boiling water and leave for 20 minutes to rehydrate. When plump and aromatic, strain, then add the soaking liquid to the hot stock.

Put the butter into a large, heavy-based saucepan, heat to melt, then add the fresh mushrooms and sauté for 5 minutes, turning and stirring now and then. Remove with a slotted spoon and set aside.

Add half the olive oil to the saucepan, then the rice, onion and garlic. Cook, stirring, for 2 minutes. Add the reserved porcini mushrooms and wine and cook until absorbed, about 3 minutes. Add 1 ladle (about 250 ml) of hot stock, let it bubble, then stir gently occasionally. Continue adding ladles of stock at 5–6 minute intervals or until the rice is tender and the stock has all been used, about 25 minutes in all – return the cooked mushrooms to the pan and add the grated Parmesan to the risotto after the third ladle.

Add salt to taste (cautiously, since the grated cheese is also salty). Sprinkle over the reserved 3 tablespoons oil, turn off the heat and serve, topped with shavings of Parmesan.

**Note** Italian risotto rice comes in many grades; carnaroli, arborio and vialone nano are three examples. Risotto rice can absorb lots of liquid (up to 4 times its volume), yet still stays *al dente* as well as creamy. It is delectable.

To make the stock, put all the stock ingredients, except the salt, into a large saucepan. Add 1.5 litres cold water, bring to the boil and simmer for about 10–15 minutes. Skim several times. Strain back into the rinsed pan and continue simmering for about 15–20 minutes. Season to taste.

To prepare the squid, gently pull the head and tentacles away from the body. Cut off and reserve the tentacles from the head section. Remove and discard the plastic-like stiffener and soft interior from the body. Remove the skin if preferred.

Discard any open or heavy mussels. Put into a saucepan with the white wine. Boil fiercely, covered, until they open (about 1–2 minutes). Remove them one by one and set aside. Strain the liquid into the stock, producing 1.5 litres.

Heat half the oil in a large paella pan or frying pan. Add the prawns, langoustines and squid and fry briefly until barely set. Remove and set aside. Add the chicken and chorizo and brown over moderate heat for 10–12 minutes.

Add the onion, pepper, garlic, tomatoes, stock and half the paprika. Bring to a rapid boil, stir in the rice, reduce the heat to a gentle simmer, and cook, uncovered, without stirring, for 16–18 minutes or until the rice is cooked.

Add the broad beans, saffron, the remaining paprika and oil. Stir, add all the seafood, then cook for 8–10 minutes on a very low heat until the rice is fully cooked and dry. Add extra stock or water as necessary. Serve, sprinkled with parsley, if using.

# spanish paella
## with chicken and seafood

Paella is a great one-pan dish. Use a round, short grain Spanish paella rice or an Italian risotto rice. Allow two handfuls, or 75–100 g per person, and cook for about 18 minutes (or 25–30 minutes for calasparra, which may also need more water).

**8 small squid***

**1 kg live mussels, scrubbed**

**150 ml white wine**

**6 tablespoons extra virgin olive oil**

**16 uncooked, unpeeled medium prawns, with heads removed and reserved for stock (see below)**

**8 uncooked langoustines**

**500 g chicken cut into chunks**

**750 g chorizo, cut into chunks**

**1 large Spanish onion, sliced**

**2 red peppers, deseeded and sliced**

**1 whole head of garlic, trimmed**

**2 large, fleshy tomatoes, chopped**

**2 teaspoons sweet paprika**

**500 g paella rice or risotto rice**

**250 g shelled and skinned broad beans**

**a pinch of saffron threads**

**6 tablespoons scissor-snipped, fresh, flat leaf parsley, to serve (optional)**

FISH STOCK

**prawn heads (see above)**

**1 kg white fish bones or heads**

**1 large bouquet garni (sprigs of thyme, bay, flat leaf parsley, celery and orange zest, tied together)**

**2 teaspoons black peppercorns**

**1 Spanish onion, quartered**

**2 carrots, quartered**

**300 ml medium white wine**

**1–2 teaspoons sea salt**

**SERVES 8**

*Some supermarkets and fishmongers sell squid ready-cleaned.*

Good olive oil and Mediterranean vegetables produce an easy, substantial pasta dish. No long simmering here: the tiny tomato halves are oven-roasted and the cubes of aubergine salted, then sautéed, to intensify the tastes. Handfuls of basil are the final flourish. Use any dry pasta – spaghetti, penne, rigatoni and maccheroni are all good. The sauce is relatively dry and there's not much of it. It is deliberate – it works!

# sicilian spaghetti

1 aubergine, about 350 g, cut into 1 cm cubes

500 g mini plum tomatoes, halved and deseeded

125 ml extra virgin olive oil

400 g dried pasta, such as spaghettini or penne

125 ml tomato purée or juice

2 garlic cloves, chopped

sea salt and freshly ground black pepper

a large handful of basil leaves, to serve

**SERVES 4**

Bring a large saucepan of salted water to the boil, ready to add the pasta when the vegetables are half cooked.

Put the aubergine into a non-metal bowl, then add 1 teaspoon salt and set aside while you cook the tomatoes.

Pack the tomatoes, cut sides up, on an oven tray, then sprinkle with the remaining salt and 2 tablespoons of the oil. Roast in a preheated oven at 230°C (450°F) Gas 8 for 10 minutes or until wilted and aromatic.

Cook the pasta according to the packet instructions (8–12 minutes, depending on type).

Drain the aubergine and pat dry with kitchen paper. Put 4 tablespoons of the olive oil into a non-stick frying pan and heat gently. Add the aubergine and cook, stirring, over high heat until frizzled and soft, about 8 minutes.

Add the roasted tomato halves, tomato purée or juice, garlic and black pepper. Cook, stirring, for 2–3 minutes, then tear up most of the basil leaves and stir through. Test the pasta for doneness and drain through a colander.

Return to the saucepan and toss in the remaining olive oil. Divide between heated bowls, spoon over the sauce, add a few fresh basil leaves and serve.

# pasta with garlic and chilli

Pasta really is one of the easiest of all dishes. To cook it, bring a large saucepan of water to the boil, add a large pinch of salt, add the pasta, then cook at a rolling boil with the lid off until tender but still firm. Garlic and chilli make a simple sauce, while the carbonara variation is one of my favourites. too – and not at all difficult.

**350 g dried spaghetti**

**4 tablespoons extra virgin olive oil**

**1 teaspoon red chilli flakes**

**6–8 garlic cloves, finely sliced or chopped**

**2 large handfuls of young rocket leaves (optional)**

**SERVES 4–6**

Bring a large saucepan of water to a boil, add a pinch of salt, then the pasta. Cook, uncovered, until tender but firm (*al dente*). Drain through a colander, then return the pasta, with about 125 ml of the cooking liquid, to the saucepan.

Put the oil, chilli, garlic and rocket, if using, into a second saucepan, heat briefly until aromatic. Add the cooked spaghetti and the reserved cooking liquid. Toss thoroughly, then serve.

**Variation** Spaghetti alla Carbonara

My favourite version of the Roman dish of pasta with bacon and eggs is based on Elizabeth David's classic. Cook the spaghetti as in the main recipe, but do not drain. Put 25 g butter into a frying pan and heat until melted. Add 150 g chopped sliced pancetta or unsmoked bacon and cook until crisp. Drain the pasta and return it to the saucepan. Add 3 lightly beaten eggs to the bacon, stir until almost set, then transfer into the pasta. Add 25 g grated Parmesan cheese and toss well. Serve with extra Parmesan.

Homemade pasta is not as difficult as you might think, and pappardelle is easier to make than most, because you cut it into strips with a knife. Elegant ingredients such as lobster, prawns or crab will make this pasta an easy, special-occasion dish.

# pappardelle
## with seafood sauce

**180 ml extra virgin olive oil, warmed**

**500 g lobster meat, from 1 kg whole lobster, or prawn or crab meat**

**a bunch of fresh dill, chopped, about 40 g**

**a bunch of fresh chives, chopped, about 40 g**

**shredded zest and juice of 1 lemon**

**sea salt and freshly crushed black pepper**

PAPPARDELLE

**500 g tipo 00 flour (from Italian delicatessens)\***

**5 free-range medium eggs**

**2 teaspoons sea salt flakes, crushed**

**extra flour or semolina flour, for shaping**

**SERVES 4**

*\*If you make your own pasta, use this special Italian fine-grade flour. If utterly unobtainable, use plain flour instead.*

To make the Pappardelle, put the flour, eggs and sea salt flakes into a food processor. Work in bursts for about 1 minute until the mixture comes together in a crumbly mass, then into a rough ball. Knead it firmly together and remove to a floured work surface.

Knead by hand for 2 minutes, then wrap in clingfilm and chill for 1 hour. Divide the dough into 4 parts, keeping 3 still wrapped. Starting on the thickest setting of the pasta machine, roll 1 piece of dough through, 3–4 times, folding the 2 ends into the middle each time to get a plump envelope of dough and giving it a half turn each time. Lightly flour the dough on both sides.

Roll it through all the settings on the pasta machine, starting at the thickest, about 6 times in all, until you get a 1 metre length of pasta (cut it in half if it's easier). Hang this over a chair or pole to air-dry. Continue the process until all the pasta sheets are lined up. Roll up each length, then slice into 2.5 cm wide ribbons (pappardelle). Unroll, dust in semolina flour, then cut each in half, to make strips about 50 cm long. Fill a large saucepan with hot water, add a pinch of salt and bring to the boil.

Meanwhile, to make the sauce, put the oil into a heavy-based frying pan and heat gently. Add the lobster, prawn or crab meat, dill, chives, 1 tablespoon of the lemon juice, salt and pepper. Heat briefly until the flavours blend well. Leave on a very low heat to keep warm.

Add the pasta to the boiling salted water, cook for 1½ minutes, then drain through a colander. Tip the pasta into the sauce, toss with 2 wooden spoons, add the lemon zest and serve in bowls.

Soba noodles are sold in many supermarkets as well as specialist Asian food stores, often next to the ingredients for sushi. Instant dashi is sold in different forms in the same stores, but you can also make your own using kombu seaweed and bonito flakes.

# soba noodles
## chilled japanese buckwheat noodles

**250 g dried soba noodles**

DASHI SAUCE

**350 ml hot dashi stock**

**4 tablespoons soy sauce**

**2 tablespoons mirin (Japanese sweet rice wine)**

**2 tablespoons caster sugar**

TO SERVE

**8 spring onions, finely sliced, plus the green tops, to serve (optional)**

**2 teaspoons wasabi paste**

**2 sheets dried nori seaweed**

**1 teaspoon black sesame seeds**

**SERVES 4**

Bring a large saucepan of water to the boil, add the noodles, return to the boil, then add a cup of cold water. Return to the boil again, then add another cup of cold water. Return to the boil for a third time, then drain, refresh and chill.

Put the dashi sauce ingredients into a bowl, stir well, then divide between 4 soup bowls. Put the spring onions into 4 side bowls, with ½ teaspoon wasabi paste beside.

Take the nori sheets, one by one, in a pair of tongs and wave over a low gas flame or hot element until they smell toasty and feel crisp, about 45 seconds. Crumble or cut into shreds. Add the shreds to the noodles, sprinkle with sesame seeds and serve with spring onion tops, if using.

Dried wheat noodles are made from flour and eggs, often sold in tightly packed yellow bundles, usually about 8 per 500 g pack. They should be soaked in hot (not boiling) water for 10 minutes to soften evenly, then be untangled and added to a saucepan of boiling salted water with 1 tablespoon peanut oil to prevent sticking or boiling over. Cooking time should be about 3–5 minutes.

# combination chow mein

**500 g dried wheat noodles**

**4 tablespoons peanut oil**

**6–8 slices rindless smoked bacon, chopped**

**250 g cooked, peeled prawns**

**4 tablespoons sweet chilli sauce**

**1 tablespoon hoisin sauce**

**4 garlic cloves, sliced**

**2.5 cm fresh ginger, finely sliced into strips**

**2–3 small heads of bok choy, separated into leaves**

**4 tablespoons light soy sauce**

**SERVES 4**

Soak the noodles in hot water, then cook and drain as described above. Heat the oil in a wok, add the bacon and prawns and stir-fry until the prawns are hot and the bacon crisp.

Add the chilli sauce, hoisin sauce, garlic, ginger and bok choy, then stir and toss for about 2 minutes, until all the ingredients are hot and crisply tender. Add the still-hot, cooked, drained noodles and the soy sauce. Stir-fry and toss until the noodles are well-coated, then serve immediately.

**Note**  Some brands of instant dried wheat noodles need only one soak-and-cook stage – follow the packet instructions.

*Mee krob* is the classic Thai dish that ideally requires a large wok, a pair of tongs and a ventilator fan. But care, optimism and an open window will do – and don't try to cook more than one skein of dried vermicelli noodles at a time. Buy the noodles, rice vinegar, fish sauce, *tom yam* stock cubes and tiny, fiercely hot, bird's eye chillies from Chinese or South-east Asian markets.

# crispy thai noodles
## with chicken, prawns, chillies, and coriander

250 g fine rice vermicelli noodles

peanut oil, for deep-frying

3 eggs, beaten

100–125 g caster sugar

4 tablespoons rice vinegar

4 tablespoons light soy sauce

4 tablespoons Thai fish sauce

100 ml spicy stock, such as stock made from *tom yam* soup stock cubes

1 tablespoon mild paprika

2 teaspoons coriander seeds, crushed

250 g uncooked prawns, peeled and deveined

4 skinless, boneless chicken breasts, finely sliced

175 g fresh beansprouts

6 spring onions, sliced lengthways

3–4 bird's eye chillies, sliced crossways

a bunch of fresh coriander, chopped

**SERVES 4–6**

Separate the layered skeins of noodles without breaking them. (Cook 1 skein at a time.) Pour about 5 cm peanut oil into a large wok and heat to 190°C (375°F), or until a single strand of noodle will puff up immediately. Set a large metal sieve over a heatproof bowl. Put crumpled kitchen paper onto a tray, ready for draining the fried noodles.

Using tongs, add a skein of noodles to the very hot oil. Cook for 10–15 seconds until puffed up and slightly browned, then turn it over carefully with tongs. Cook the second side, then set it on the kitchen paper. Repeat until all the noodles have been cooked. If there is any dark debris in the oil, pour all the oil through the sieve into the heatproof bowl, discard the debris and return the oil to the wok. Reheat and continue cooking the remaining noodles. Pour out the hot oil, return the cooked noodles to the empty wok and keep them warm.

Heat a small frying pan, add 1 tablespoon of hot oil, then half the eggs. Cook the omelette briefly on both sides. Remove and repeat with the remaining mixture. Roll up the omelettes, slice into strips and set aside.

Wipe out the pan and add the sugar, rice vinegar, soy and fish sauces, stock, paprika and coriander. Heat, stirring, until syrupy. Add the prawns and poach until firm. Remove and set aside. Cook the chicken in the same way. Increase the heat, add the beansprouts, spring onions, omelette and prawns and toss gently. Tip the mixture over the hot noodles in the large wok. Turn the noodles to coat, breaking them as little as possible. Add the chillies and coriander, then serve hot.

chicken,

# fish & meat

# spicy thai chicken soup

One of the world's best-loved soups. Ingredients like lemongrass and kaffir lime leaves are sold in supermarkets as part of the packs of fresh Thai herbs and flavourings. You could use lemon and lime zest instead if you can't find them. Just don't use dried versions from the spice rack – they're just not good enough. Buy extra of the fresh ingredients and freeze them for later.

Put the stock into a large saucepan and bring to the boil. Add the chicken, garlic, lemongrass, fish sauce or light soy sauce, ginger, spring onions and creamed coconut.

Return to the boil, part-cover, reduce the heat to a high simmer and cook for 5 minutes. Add the kaffir lime leaves, if using, the chillies, half the coriander and the prawns.

Simmer gently for 5 minutes or until the chicken is cooked through and the prawn flesh is densely white – do not overcook or the prawns will be tough. Add the lime juice and serve in heated soup bowls, topped with the remaining coriander leaves.

**Note**  Remove the chillies before drinking the soup: they are fiery, but leaving them whole and merely crushing them releases a gentle, not violent, heat.

**1.25 litres boiling chicken stock, preferably homemade**

**350 g boneless, skinless chicken breasts, finely sliced**

**2 garlic cloves, chopped**

**2 stalks of lemongrass, halved lengthways**

**3 tablespoons fish sauce or light soy sauce**

**6 cm fresh ginger, peeled and grated**

**8 small spring onions, quartered**

**50 g creamed coconut, chopped**

**4 fresh kaffir lime leaves, crushed (optional)**

**2 green bird's eye chillies, crushed**

**a large handful of fresh coriander leaves, torn**

**250 g uncooked tiger prawns, tails only, peeled or unpeeled***

**freshly squeezed juice of 2 limes**

**SERVES 4: MAKES 1.5 LITRES**

*Do not use cooked prawns: the texture will be disappointing. Use cubes of other fresh fish instead.*

# chicken kebabs

Small, barbecued chicken pieces, sliced and wrapped with herbs, salad and dressing, must be one of the easiest party ideas known. Flour tortillas, lavash and pita breads make the best wraps, but any flatbread will do.

Push the chicken onto the skewers and set in a large, shallow, non-metal tray or container. Mix the oil, oregano, salt, pepper and lemon juice in a jug, then pour the mixture over the chicken. Let marinate for 10 minutes. Heat a barbecue or grill and cook the kebabs for 5–8 minutes on each side or until the chicken is firm and white right through.

Put the grated cucumber into a sieve and squeeze it dry. Put into a bowl and mix with the yoghurt, garlic, mint or parsley and salt. Gently warm the bread and, if using pita bread, cut in half and open out the pocket.

Pull the cooked chicken off the skewers and divide between the breads, add the sliced cucumber, tomatoes, lettuce and onion, spoon in some yoghurt mixture and herb sprigs, and fold, wrap or roll up. Serve. (Wrap in paper for easy handling.)

500 g boneless chicken breasts and thighs, cut into 2 cm cubes

4 tablespoons extra virgin olive oil

1 teaspoon dried oregano

½ teaspoon sea salt

1 teaspoon cracked black pepper

freshly squeezed juice of 1 lemon

TO SERVE

20 cm cucumber, half sliced, half grated coarsely

125 ml thick plain yoghurt

2 garlic cloves, chopped

4 tablespoons chopped fresh mint or flat leaf parsley, plus extra sprigs, to serve

½–1 teaspoon salt, to taste

4 flatbreads such as flour tortillas, lavash or halved pita bread

1–2 tomatoes, diced

½ head crisp lettuce, such as cos, chopped

1 red onion, sliced into rings

*4 metal kebab skewers, oiled, or 8 bamboo satay sticks, soaked in water for 30 minutes*

**SERVES 4**

Almost all the world appreciates this dish. Stir-fried also means 'steam-stirred' in my book, because the vegetables mostly cook in the aromatic steam. Use a sweet chilli sauce, not a fiery South-east Asian version.

# stir-fried chicken with greens

Put the oil into a wok and heat until very hot but not smoking. Alternatively, use a large, preferably non-stick, frying pan. Add the chicken and stir-fry over a high heat for 2 minutes, then add the ginger and garlic and stir-fry for a further 2 minutes.

Add the prepared broccoli, spring onions, green beans, sliced pepper and chicken stock or water. Cover and cook for a further 2–3 minutes. Stir in the chilli sauce and soy sauce. Toss the still-wet mangetout, sugar snap peas and bok choy leaves on top. Cover and cook for 1–2 minutes. Toss well and serve while the tastes and colours are still vivid and the textures crisp.

**2 tablespoons peanut oil**

**500 g chicken breasts, cubed, or 3 large skinless, boneless breasts cut into 5 cm strips or cubes**

**5 cm fresh ginger, shredded**

**2 garlic cloves, sliced**

**250 g broccoli, broken into tiny florets**

**8 spring onions, halved crossways**

**175 g green beans, halved and blanched in boiling salted water**

**1 red or yellow pepper, deseeded and cut into strips**

**6 tablespoons chicken stock or water**

**2 tablespoons sweet chilli sauce**

**1 tablespoon light soy sauce**

**50 g mangetout (snowpeas), trimmed and washed**

**50 g sugar snap peas, trimmed and washed**

**100 g baby bok choy leaves, trimmed and washed**

**noodles or rice, to serve**

**SERVES 4**

# thai green chicken curry

This green Thai curry is now one of the world's favourite dishes. Spice pastes – red, green, orange mussaman and so on – are an intrinsic part of Thai cooking. This classic green spice paste makes the amount you'll need in this recipe, but you could use it for other Thai dishes as well. If time is short, buy ready-made pastes in larger supermarkets and South-east Asian or Chinese food markets, but add a handful of fresh coriander, too. The food processor makes spice mix preparation a work of seconds, but use a mortar and pestle if you prefer.

2 tablespoons peanut oil

4 skinless chicken breasts, about 800 g, quartered crossways

150 ml chicken stock

500 ml canned coconut milk

125 g Thai 'pea' aubergines or diced cucumber

1 teaspoon fish sauce or 1 teaspoon salt

freshly squeezed juice of 1 lime

a large bunch of mint

boiled fragrant Thai rice, to serve

GREEN CURRY PASTE

2–3 medium hot green chillies, deseeded and finely sliced

a bunch of coriander, chopped, about 30 g

2 stalks of lemongrass, finely sliced

3 cm fresh ginger, peeled and finely sliced

2 fresh kaffir lime leaves, shredded hair-thin, or 1 tablespoon freshly grated lime zest

1 teaspoon coriander seeds, crushed

½ teaspoon cumin seeds, crushed

2 spring onions, chopped, or small red onions

2 garlic cloves, crushed

**SERVES 4**

Put all the Green Curry Paste ingredients into a food processor and grind to a smooth paste. Alternatively, use a mortar and pestle. If using ready-made spice paste, add the chopped coriander.

Put the oil into a large, preferably non-stick, frying pan or wok, heat gently, then add the chicken and sauté for 2–3 minutes or until firm and golden. Turn the pieces over as they cook.

Add the reserved curry paste. Sauté, stirring, for 1 minute. Add the chicken stock and return to the boil.

Add half the coconut milk and the pea aubergines or cucumber and cook, covered, at a rapid simmer (don't let boil) for 5 minutes. Using tongs, turn the chicken pieces over, then reduce the heat to a very gentle simmer. Add the remaining coconut milk and the fish sauce or salt and cook, uncovered, for a further 8–12 minutes.

Add the lime juice and sprinkle with mint. Serve with fragrant Thai rice.

Piri-piri refers to the tiny, searingly hot fresh or dried chillies infused in vinegar, giving a fiery condiment. It is an idea that turns up all over the world and is nice and easy. No chillies? Then add a dash of Tabasco: easiest of all.

# chicken piri-piri

To prepare the poussins, cut them in half down the back and cut out and discard the backbone. Cut down each breast. Beat each half out flat with a the flat of a cleaver or meat mallet. Pat dry with kitchen paper. Set on an oven tray with the potato and orange wedges tucked in and around them. Slash the skin twice on the outer curve of each leg (thigh and drumstick). Put the garlic, orange cubes, oil and salt into a blender and purée for 30 seconds. Pour the mixture over the chicken, orange and potatoes.

Bake, uncovered, in a preheated oven at 180°C (350°F) Gas 4 for 20 minutes, then increase the heat to 200°C (400°F) Gas 6. Continue cooking for a further 15–25 minutes or until the poussins and potatoes are done. (Pierce the meat near the bone – it should be opaque right through and no longer pink.)

Meanwhile, to make the Piri-piri Dressing, put the vinegar, chillies (pierced with a cocktail stick if fresh), peppercorns and wine into a screwtop bottle with a plastic nozzle (just like you see in all the cafés). Shake well to mix.

Remove the poussins, potatoes and orange wedges from the oven, transfer to a serving platter and spoon over the pan juices. Serve the Piri-piri Dressing separately.

**2 poussins, about 400–450 g each**

**6 potatoes, cut into wedges**

**1 whole orange, unpeeled, half cut into wedges, half into 1 cm cubes**

**4 garlic cloves, crushed**

**6 tablespoons extra virgin olive oil**

**1 teaspoon salt**

**green salad, to serve**

PIRI-PIRI DRESSING

**250 ml red wine vinegar**

**25–30 g fresh, hot red chillies or 15 g dried**

**1 teaspoon black peppercorns**

**125 ml port, Madeira wine or dry sherry**

**SERVES 4**

# chicken tagine
## with apricots

½ teaspoon ground turmeric

½–1 teaspoon saffron powder

1.5 kg chicken, cut into 8 or 10 pieces

250 g dried apricots

3 tablespoons butter or olive oil

2 onions, chopped

½ teaspoon ground ginger

½ teaspoon paprika

½ teaspoon crushed black peppercorns

1 teaspoon salt

a handful of fresh parsley, tied with string

1 cooking apple such as Granny Smith, cored but not peeled, then cut into 8 pieces

sprigs of mint, to serve (optional)

**SERVES 4**

This simple chicken dish uses only five spices: two of which are used to rub into the skin of the chicken. If you can't find real saffron powder, double the amount of paprika and use half of that to help colour the chicken. The apricots grow plump and juicy with blanching and give the dish a good balance of sweet, salty and sour flavours.

Mix the turmeric with the saffron, then rub it all over the chicken pieces. Put the apricots into a small saucepan, add 250 ml boiling water, bring very gently to the boil, cover with a lid, then simmer for about 10 minutes.

Heat the butter or oil in a large flameproof casserole, add the onions and sauté for 5 minutes, stirring. Add the ginger, paprika, peppercorns and salt. Put the chicken on top.

Add 350 ml cold water to the apricots, then pour the apricots and their liquid over and around the chicken.

Add the parsley, bring to the boil, cover with a lid, then reduce to a simmer and cook, undisturbed, for 20 minutes. Add the apple. Simmer gently for a further 10–15 minutes, adding a little extra water if it looks too dry (the fruit absorbs much of the water).

Remove and discard the parsley. Serve the tagine with couscous or plain rice, topped with a few mint sprigs, if using.

# provençal roasted chicken
## with garlic, lemons and olives

Roasted chicken is everyone's favourite. Add garlic, olives and thyme and it suddenly acquires all the flavours of the Mediterranean. Easy and delicious, and special enough for a casual dinner party.

1.25–1.5 kg free range, corn fed chicken

3 tablespoons extra virgin olive oil

2 lemons

a large bunch of fresh thyme

175 g black olives, preferably dry-cured

4 whole heads of garlic

125 ml full-bodied red wine (optional)

sea salt and freshly ground black pepper

**SERVES 4**

Pat the chicken dry with kitchen paper. Rub the skin with a little olive oil and sprinkle with salt inside and out. Put, breast side down, into a roasting tin.

Slice the lemons crossways in a series of parallel slashes, but leave them attached at the base. Put half the thyme and one of the lemons inside the cavity and push more thyme between the trussed legs and underneath the bird. Push the olives under the bird. Add the remaining lemon to the roasting tin.

Slice a 'lid' off the top of each head of garlic. Spread 1 teaspoon olive oil over each one and replace the lids. Brush the remaining oil over the chicken and lemon.

Roast the chicken, breast side down, in a preheated oven at 220°C (425°F) Gas 7 for 40 minutes. Turn the bird on its back. Remove the prepared garlic and set aside. Roast the bird for a further 35–40 minutes until deep golden brown. Prick the thigh at the thickest part – the juices should run a clear yellow (use a metal spoon to check the colour). If there is any trace of pink, roast a little longer. Remove the chicken and olives from the pan. Let stand, covered, in a warm place for 8–10 minutes while you make the sauce (optional).

To make the sauce, pour off the pan juices from the tin. Measure 25 ml of the stickiest, darkest juices and put into a blender or food processor. Add the red wine. Press the soft, creamy centres out of the garlic heads and add to the blender. Tip up the bird and let the juices run into the blender or food processor. Add a quarter of the roasted lemon, pulled into pieces. Blend, in bursts, to a rich sauce. Taste and add water if necessary. Gently simmer until the raw taste of wine has mellowed, about 3–5 minutes. Serve with the chicken.

This famous American seafood soup is not at all complicated. Use whatever clams, mussels and other seafood are available locally. Even canned clams – in or out of their shells – added at the end of the cooking time, will do if you can't find fresh ones.

# spicy clam chowder

Put half the olive oil into a large frying pan, heat gently, then add the bacon and sauté until crisp. Remove with a slotted spoon. Add the clams and half the stock. Cover the pan and bring to the boil. Reduce the heat and simmer for 5 minutes or until the clams open.

Put wet muslin or wet kitchen paper into a sieve and pour the clams and their liquid through the sieve to strain out the sand. Reserve the cooking liquid and the clams.

Put the remaining oil into the rinsed pan, heat gently, then add the onion, potatoes, celery, paprika and chilli and sauté for 5 minutes. Add the tomatoes, remaining stock and salt. Bring to the boil, reduce the heat and simmer for 10 minutes or until the vegetables are part-tender. Add the reserved cooking liquid, bacon and clams, stir gently, then simmer for 5–10 minutes, until the flavours are well blended. Serve in deep, wide soup bowls, with parsley sprinkled on top.

**Note** Saltines (salted, crisp crackers) are the traditional accompaniment, but any salted crackers will do. French bread or crusty rolls are also suitable.

4 tablespoons extra virgin olive oil

4 slices bacon, cut into strips or large dice, about 75 g

1 kg live clams, well scrubbed

750 ml boiling fish stock or chicken stock

1 large onion, chopped

2–4 medium potatoes, cubed, about 400 g

3 celery stalks, sliced

2 teaspoons hot paprika

1 medium-hot red chilli, deseeded and chopped

400 g canned chopped tomatoes

1 teaspoon sea salt flakes

leaves from a small bunch of flat leaf parsley, chopped

**SERVES 6–8**

This simple mixture of parsley, garlic and extra virgin olive oil can create a superb, vividly scented green oil which will make any seafood taste good. Sprinkled over sizzled scallops, prawns or fish, it's a sensational recipe altogether.

# char-grilled scallops
## with parsley oil

Mix the garlic, oil and lemon juice in a shallow, non-metal dish. Pat the scallops dry with kitchen paper. Make shallow crisscross cuts in each one, 3 times each way on each side. Prick the corals with a toothpick to prevent splitting. Add the scallops to the dish of marinade, turning once and set aside while you prepare the parsley oil.

Put the parsley, oil and garlic into a blender and blend until smooth. Strain into a bowl or just pour straight from the blender and use this vivid green oil as both garnish and condiment.

Drain the scallops, then thread onto the skewers, 2 per skewer. Pour the marinade into a frying pan, bring to the boil and cook until reduced to a sticky golden glaze. Add the scallops and sizzle them in the glaze for 1 minute each side (or a little longer if preferred). Serve, sprinkled with parsley oil and a separate small dish of oil for dipping. Sprinkle with salt and pepper and decorate with a bundle of chives, if using.

**Variation** If you prefer to barbecue or grill the scallops, put the skewers onto an oiled rack about 5–6 cm from a very hot barbecue or grill. Sizzle until firm and golden, 3–5 minutes. Put the marinade into a saucepan, bring to the boil and cook until reduced to a sticky glaze.

**Note** Always try to buy fresh local scallops on the shell and get your fishmonger to prepare them. If buying scallops out of the shell, don't buy any that are sitting in water. The water soaks into the flesh and the minute they hit the pan the water exudes and the result is a stew, rather than a grill.

**2 garlic cloves, crushed**

**4 tablespoons extra virgin olive oil**

**juice of 1 lemon**

**375–400 g fresh scallops, about 16**

**sea salt and freshly ground black pepper**

**a small handful of fresh chives, to serve (optional)**

PARSLEY OIL

**a small bunch of flat leaf parsley, finely chopped, about 15 g**

**125 ml extra virgin olive oil**

**1 garlic clove, crushed**

*8 short wooden skewers or satay sticks, soaked in water for 30 minutes*

**SERVES 4**

# spicy char-grilled prawns

This homemade spice mix has lots of flavour, without too much heat. Spices are always better freshly ground – I give a suggested combination below. Alternatively, go to an Asian store where spice mixes are freshly made.

**1 kg large, uncooked tiger prawns, shell-on (about 16)**

SPICE MIX

**2 tablespoons mild or hot paprika**

**1 teaspoon kashmiri dried chillies, crushed**

**4 tablespoons garam masala (see note)**

**2 teaspoons ground turmeric**

**1 teaspoons coriander seeds, crushed**

**1 tablespoon sea salt flakes**

**5 cm fresh ginger, peeled and grated**

**4 garlic cloves, crushed**

**125 g ghee or clarified butter, melted**

**2 limes**

*8 wooden or bamboo skewers, soaked in water for about 30 minutes*

**MAKES 8: SERVES 4**

Slash the curved backs of the prawns, then remove and discard any black threads. Pat the prawns dry with kitchen paper. Grind the paprika, dried chillies, garam masala, turmeric, coriander and salt with a mortar and pestle or electric spice grinder. Add the ginger and garlic, then grind to a rough powdery paste. Add the ghee or butter and juice of one of the limes. Stir well. Rub the mixture into the prawns, pushing it under the shells so it penetrates the flesh.

Thread 2 prawns onto each skewer, then grill or barbecue over low heat until aromatic: the flesh should be white and firm and the shells pink. Serve with the remaining lime, cut into wedges.

**Note** To make a fresh garam masala, mix 2 tablespoons each of crushed cinnamon, cumin seeds and coriander seeds in a small frying pan. Add 1 tablespoon each of the seeds from green cardamom pods, peppercorns, cloves and ground mace. Dry-toast to release the aromas, then cool, grind in a spice grinder and either use immediately or store in a jar with a tight-fitting lid.

The only time-consuming aspect of this relaxed recipe is pre-soaking and desalting the bacalau (salt cod). Its superb taste is the classic base for these fish cakes. You can also use smoked cod, smoked haddock or even half fresh salmon mixed with half smoked salmon instead. Put the salt cod, if using, into a bowl, cover with cold water, refrigerate for 24 hours, changing the water every 8 hours. Easy!

Cook the potatoes in boiling salted water for 20 minutes. Drain well, return to the still-hot empty saucepan and let dry.

Put the milk into a frying pan, bring to the boil, add the fish and poach gently until flaking and hot, about 6–8 minutes. Drain well, reserving the hot milk. Cool the fish, then skin, bone and flake it.

Add the flaked fish to the saucepan, then the extra virgin olive oil, egg, spring onions, coriander, salt and pepper. Mix and mash to a dense texture, adding ½–1 tablespoon of the hot milk if necessary. Divide the mixture into 8–12 balls. Pat out into flat cakes, then coat in the seasoned flour.

Put most of the olive oil into a non-stick frying pan and heat to 190°C (375°F) or until a 1 cm cube of bread browns in 35–45 seconds. Cook 3–4 fish cakes at a time for 4 minutes on each side. Using a spatula and a slotted spoon, turn them carefully to avoid splashes. Drain on crumpled kitchen paper and keep hot while all the rest are cooked, adding the extra oil to the pan. Serve hot with lime or lemon wedges.

**500 g floury potatoes, halved lengthways**

**350 ml full-cream milk**

**350 g smoked haddock or cod, or desalted salt cod**

**2 tablespoons extra virgin olive oil**

**1 egg, beaten**

**4 spring onions, chopped**

**a small bunch of fresh coriander, chopped, about 25 g**

**8 tablespoons plain flour, to coat**

**6–8 tablespoons virgin olive oil, for frying**

**sea salt and freshly ground black pepper**

**lemon or lime wedges, to serve**

**SERVES 4**

spanish fish cakes

Steaming a fish is a wonderfully easy idea. This recipe tastes superb, too, and looks beautiful. When serving the fish, lift off the top fillets first, then remove and discard the backbone before serving the rest of the fillets. This is a traditional cooking technique often used in China, Japan and South-east Asia.

# steamed bass with leeks and ginger

Pat the fish dry, inside and out, with kitchen paper. Make 5–6 diagonal slashes right to the bone on both sides of the fish. Rub salt and sesame oil into the slashes and around the cavity. Set the fish on a heatproof dish which will fit neatly into the steamer basket, but still allow the steam to circulate.

Cut the spring onions in half crossways, then finely slice lengthways. Cut the leek into similar pieces. Peel the ginger and cut it into fine matchstick julienne strips. Scatter the leek, ginger and half the spring onions over the fish, pushing some inside the cavity.

Put the fish into a steamer set over a wok or pan of boiling water, cover and cook at high heat for about 15–20 minutes. Do not let boil dry – top up with more boiling water if necessary. Remove the fish. Put the soy sauce, rice wine or sherry and peanut oil into a bowl, mix well, then pour over the fish. Sprinkle with the reserved spring onions and serve.

**2 medium sea bass or grey mullet, well cleaned (about 750 g)**

**1 teaspoon salt**

**2 teaspoons sesame oil**

**4 spring onions**

**1 small leek**

**7.5 cm fresh ginger**

**2 tablespoons light soy sauce**

**2 tablespoons Chinese rice wine or sherry**

**2 tablespoons peanut oil**

**SERVES 4**

This spicy barbecued pork is eaten with the fingers or with bread rolls or dumplings. Its distinctive flavour is allspice, also known as Jamaican pepper or pimento. Traditionally, jerk pork is cooked over coals made from the wood of this native Jamaican allspice tree, but if you have to use an ordinary barbecue or overhead grill, it will still taste very good.

# jamaican jerk pork with herb dumplings

**4 tablespoons tomato ketchup**

**4 tablespoons fresh lime or lemon juice**

**2 tablespoons dark soy sauce**

**1 tablespoon Barbados or brown sugar**

**1 teaspoon coarsely ground black peppercorns**

**1 teaspoon allspice berries, crushed**

**½ teaspoon chilli powder**

**½ teaspoon grated lime zest**

**3 garlic cloves, finely chopped**

**1 teaspoon salt, or to taste**

**675 g boneless pork loin, chops or steaks, patted dry with kitchen paper**

**200 g plain flour**

**50 g dried milk powder**

**1 teaspoon baking powder**

**½ teaspoon salt**

**4 tablespoons chopped fresh flat leaf parsley**

**corn oil, for frying**

**SERVES 4**

Put the ketchup, citrus juice and soy sauce into a shallow, non-metal dish, then stir in the sugar, peppercorns, allspice, chilli powder, lime zest, garlic and salt. Add the pork and set aside for 1 hour.

To make the herb dumplings, put all the dry ingredients and the parsley into a bowl, mix well, then stir in 200 ml water. Shape the dough into balls using 2 dessertspoons. Fill a saucepan one-third full with corn oil and heat to 180°C (350°F) or until a cube of bread browns in 40 seconds. Deep-fry until crispy outside and fluffy inside. Drain on crumpled kitchen paper.

Barbecue the pork over high heat for 2 minutes on each side. Alternatively, cook under a very hot grill. Serve plain or with the dumplings or rolls.

# spicy pork with mexican recado sauce

Many Mexican recipes for pork, especially pork loin or tenderloin fillet, use a spicy mix to add flavour, colour and sometimes tenderness. Pork can be sliced and used in whatever way you choose: in salad, on rice, in tortillas, wrapped in leaves or on a purée of sweet potato or pumpkin or with grilled vine tomatoes.

**750 g pork loin, cut into 2 cm slices**

**1½ tablespoons fruit or cider vinegar**

**6 tablespoons extra virgin olive oil**

RECADO

**1 red onion, cut crossways
into 1 cm slices**

**4 garlic cloves, peeled**

**1 tablespoon hot red paprika**

**1 tablespoon annatto powder (optional)**

**1 teaspoon allspice berries**

**1 teaspoon black peppercorns**

**2 teaspoons coarse crystal salt**

**1 teaspoon dried oregano, pan-toasted**

**SERVES 3–4**

Pat the meat dry with kitchen paper. Put the vinegar and half the olive oil into a cup and stir. Put the meat into a large plastic bag, add the olive oil mixture and shake to coat. Set aside to marinate in the refrigerator for at least 30 minutes or up to 2 hours.

To make the Recado, put the onion and garlic into a preheated, non-stick frying pan or stove-top grill pan. Cook dry (without oil) until toasty, dark and soft. Put the onion and garlic into a food processor, then add the paprika, annatto, if using, allspice, peppercorns, salt and oregano and grind to a thick paste. Alternatively, use a mortar and pestle.

Pour the marinade out of the plastic bag into a bowl. Add the paste to the bag, then knead and rub it into the meat until all surfaces are coated.

Preheat a barbecue or overhead grill until very hot. Remove the meat from the bag and grill or char-grill about 5 cm from the heat for 8–10 minutes on each side, then serve hot or cold.

# rack of lamb
## with roasted baby vegetables

Racks of lamb are chined and French-trimmed when you buy them – if not, get the butcher to do it for you. The lamb is roasted with baby vegetables and served simply with fresh herbs. Perfect dinner party fare and easy on the cook, too, because there are no bones to carve.

**2 racks of lamb, about 300 g each, French-trimmed and chined by the butcher, and all fat removed**

**1 tablespoon cracked black pepper**

**2 teaspoons dark soy sauce**

**1 tablespoon sun-dried tomato paste**

**125 ml extra virgin olive oil**

**350 g baby new potatoes, scrubbed well and halved lengthways**

**350 g butternut squash or pumpkin, cut into 1 cm chunks**

**4–6 tablespoons red wine**

**4 sprigs of fresh herbs, such as mint, parsley or rosemary**

**sea salt flakes, crushed**

**SERVES 4**

Pat the lamb dry with kitchen paper. Put the pepper into a small bowl, add the soy sauce, sun-dried tomato paste and 1 tablespoon of the oil and mix to a purée. Brush or rub the mixture all over the lamb. Set aside in a cool place or the refrigerator while you prepare the vegetables.

Put the potatoes, cut side down, and the squash or pumpkin into a shallow roasting tin. Leave at least a quarter of the area clear for the lamb to be added later. Sprinkle the remaining olive oil over the vegetables and sprinkle with about 1 tablespoon crushed sea salt flakes.

Roast towards the top of a preheated oven at 200°C (400°F) Gas 6 for 30 minutes. Add the 2 racks of lamb, side by side, with the bones pointing upwards. Continue roasting for a further 20–25 minutes or until the outside is brown, the inside faintly pink.

Remove the lamb from the oven and let it rest in a warm place for 5–10 minutes to set the juices. Add the red wine to the juices and sediment remaining in the roasting tin. Heat on top of the stove, stirring frequently, until reduced to a sauce.

Arrange piles of vegetables on 4 heated dinner plates. Slice the lamb into cutlets, stack 3–4 on each plate with the bones upwards, sprinkle with herbs, then serve with a little sauce spooned around the meat.

Rub 1 tablespoon of the oil into the steak, then rub in the garlic. Let stand for up to 1 hour to develop the flavours. Put the remaining oil into a bowl, then stir in the red wine, balsamic vinegar, salt and pepper to make a dressing.

Heat a barbecue, grill or stove-top grill pan until very hot. Put the steak diagonally onto the surface and let sizzle for 2 minutes, pressing down occasionally (the heat must be intense). Turn the steak over and cook for 2 minutes more or until aromatic and firm, but still rare. Remove the pan from the heat, cover with foil and set aside in a warm place for 2 minutes.

Toss the rocket leaves, onion and herbs in half the dressing and divide between 4 plates. Carve the steak into thin slices and keep all the juices. Pile the meat on top of the greens, stir the steak juices into the remaining dressing, then sprinkle over each serving. Serve with crusty country bread.

**6 tablespoons extra virgin olive oil**

**1 aged rump steak, about 1 kg, 2 cm thick**

**4 garlic cloves, crushed**

**2 tablespoons red wine**

**2 teaspoons balsamic vinegar**

**4 large handfuls of baby rocket or watercress**

**1 red onion, finely sliced into rings**

**a small handful of fresh chives, parsley or chervil, or a mixture of these**

**salt and freshly ground black pepper**

**SERVES 4**

# sliced beef on a bed of rocket

Use the best-quality beef available to produce this tender, char-grilled, rare-cooked steak teamed with bitter rocket leaves or peppery watercress.

Stews and casseroles aren't difficult: put them on to cook and they look after themselves. This one makes a useful two-course meal. Serve some of the juices poured over pasta as a first course, then proceed to the meat proper as a main course. Like most stews, it actually improves if made the day before then reheated. Easy entertaining.

# boeuf en daube

Cut the beef into pieces about the size of 'half a postcard', as Elizabeth David advised – in other words, 6 cm squares. Heat the oil in a large, flameproof casserole, add the garlic, bacon, carrots and onions and sauté for 4–5 minutes, or until aromatic. Remove from the casserole. Put a layer of meat into the casserole, then add half the sautéed vegetable mixture and a second layer of meat. Add the remaining vegetable mixture, the tomatoes, orange zest, herbs and walnuts.

Put the wine into a small saucepan and bring to the boil. Add the Cognac or brandy and warm for a few seconds, shaking the pan a little to let the alcohol cook away. Pour the hot liquids over the meat with just enough stock or water so that it's barely covered. Put the pork rind, if using, on top.

Heat the casserole until simmering, then cover with foil and a lid and simmer gently for 2 hours or until the meat is fork tender and the juices rich and sticky.

The dish can also be cooked in the oven. Just bring to the boil over a high heat, reduce to a simmer, cover with foil, replace the lid and cook in the oven at 160°C (325°F) Gas 3 for 2½ hours. or until very tender.

Remove and discard the rind: it will have given a velvety quality to the sauce. Sprinkle with chopped parsley. Serve hot either absolutely plain, or with accompaniments such as pasta, mashed potatoes or rice.

**Note** If using a ceramic casserole, brown the meat and vegetables in a frying pan, then transfer to the casserole. Cover with a lid and transfer to a hot oven, about 200°C (400°F) Gas 6, until the contents come to the boil, about 20–30 minutes. Reduce the heat immediately and continue as in the main recipe.

1 kg beef, such as shoulder or topside, cut into 1 cm slices

4 tablespoons extra virgin olive oil

4 garlic cloves, sliced

125 g thick-cut unsmoked bacon, cut into small dice, or bacon lardons, cubed

3 carrots, halved lengthways

12–16 baby onions, peeled

6 plum tomatoes, skinned, then thickly sliced

zest of 1 orange, removed in one piece

a bunch of fresh herbs, such as parsley, thyme, bay leaf and rosemary, tied with kitchen string

60 g walnut halves

250 ml robust red wine

2 tablespoons Cognac or brandy

150 ml beef stock or water

15 cm square of pork or bacon rind (optional)

sea salt

SERVES 4–6

sweet

things

# italian gelati

Glorious homemade ice cream is easy if you have an electric ice cream maker. If you don't, just pour the mixture into a lidded metal or plastic container and freeze for 4–6 hours, stirring the edges into the centre every hour. The texture will be less creamy, but it is still good. Flavour the basic custard in any number of ways: I've given two of my favourites here, but you could use fruit or nut liqueurs or Italian Strega liqueur.

250 ml full cream milk

160 g caster sugar

4 egg yolks

250 g mascarpone or other cream cheese

CITRUS FLAVOURING

250 ml orange juice (about 4 oranges)

250 ml lemon juice (about 5 lemons)

250 ml clementine (mandarin) juice
(about 5 clementines)

90 g caster sugar

1 tablespoon citrus liqueur
(limoncello or Cointreau)

½ teaspoon orange flower water

STRAWBERRY FLAVOURING

750 g ripe fresh strawberries

90 g caster sugar

1 tablespoon fruit liqueur or dark rum

½ teaspoon orange flower water

**MAKES 1 LITRE: SERVES 8**

To make the citrus flavouring, put the orange, lemon and clementine juices, the 90 g sugar, liqueur and orange flower water into a bowl, mix, then strain.

To make the strawberry flavouring, put the berries and the 90 g sugar into a bowl with the liqueur or rum and orange flower water, if using. Mash to a pulp. Set the bowl in a saucepan of hot water for 10 minutes. Purée in a blender, then strain through a non-metal sieve and discard the seeds.

To make the gelato base, put the milk into a saucepan and bring to the boil. Put the egg yolks and the 160 g sugar into a non-metal, heatproof bowl, whisk to a pale froth, then whisk in the hot milk. Put the bowl over a saucepan of simmering water and stir gently until smoothly creamy and thick enough to coat the back of a spoon.

Fold in the mascarpone or other cream cheese, 1 tablespoon at a time, then stir until dissolved. Put the bowl into iced water to cool, stirring now and then. When cool, fold in the citrus or strawberry flavourings. Stir until evenly mixed.

Churn and serve immediately, or transfer to a plastic, lidded container and freeze. When ready to serve, soften in the refrigerator for 25–40 minutes before serving.

# coconut ice cream

Subtle coconut ice cream with only four ingredients –
five if you count the lime zest. Heaven – and perfect for
serving after any Asian-style main course.

**500 ml milk**

**250 g caster sugar**

**500 ml unsweetened,
canned coconut milk**

**1 tablespoon dark rum
or fresh lime juice**

**lime zest or wedges,
to serve**

**SERVES 8**

Put half the milk and all the sugar into a heavy-based saucepan
and bring to the boil, stirring until dissolved. Remove from the
heat. Add the remaining milk and the coconut milk. Cool over
iced water and stir in the rum or lime juice.

Transfer to an ice-cream making machine. Churn for about
25–40 minutes, or according to the manufacturer's instructions,
until firm and silky.

Alternatively, freeze in plastic trays until the mixture is hard at
the edges, but soft in the centre. Remove and stir well, then
refreeze as before. Repeat and refreeze.

Serve in bowls, glasses or cones, topped with lime zest or with
lime wedges for squeezing.

This Spanish-style doughnut batter must cook in very hot olive oil, so that the outside crisps and seals quickly and the batter inside is cooked by steam. Add some hot chocolate for dipping and you have a wonderfully indulgent treat.

# churros with hot chocolate

**350 g self-raising flour**

**½ teaspoon salt**

**1 egg, beaten**

**400–450 ml milk**

**olive oil, for frying**

TO COAT

**8 tablespoons caster sugar**

**4 tablespoons ground cinnamon (optional)**

HOT CHOCOLATE

**250 g bitter dark chocolate, chopped or grated**

**600 ml milk, boiled**

*a piping bag with a 1–2 cm star nozzle*

**SERVES 4**

Sieve the flour and salt into a bowl. Make a well in the centre. Whisk the egg in a bowl with 250 ml of the milk. Pour into the well and whisk into the flour. Gradually whisk in enough of the remaining milk to make a smooth, creamy, thick batter able to be piped easily. Transfer the batter to a piping bag with a 1–2 cm star nozzle.

Pour a 10 cm depth of olive oil into a heavy-based saucepan fitted with a frying basket. Heat it to 190°C (375°F) or until a cube of bread browns in 35 seconds.

Pipe long, spiralled, coiled-up lengths directly into the oil. Let sizzle and cook for 4–6 minutes or until golden and spongy, not raw, in the centre (test one to check).

Lift the churros out of the oil using the basket or tongs. Drain on crumpled kitchen paper. Repeat using the remaining doughnut mixture.

When cool, scissor-snip the churros into 15 cm lengths. Put the sugar into a shallow dish, mix in the cinnamon, if using, then roll the pieces in the mixture.

To make the hot chocolate, whisk the chocolate and boiled milk together in a small saucepan, whisking and cooking until the chocolate is well blended and the liquid is dusky brown. Serve in 4 cups or bowls with the churros.

Serve these for breakfast, or with coffee in the afternoon, or as an outrageously delicious pudding accompanied by thick Greek yoghurt. Bliss!

# crisp honey fritters
## with honey syrup and cinnamon

Put the yeast, flour, sugar, salt and 250 ml lukewarm water into a bowl and mix well. Enclose in a plastic bag and leave in a warm place for 30 minutes to 2 hours, or until bubbling.

When ready to cook, take a handful of the stretchy, elastic dough. Squeeze it through the bottom of your fist and, with oiled finger and thumb of your other and, pinch out small, walnut sized pieces onto a plate. Alternatively, use 2 spoons, pincer-like, to pinch out blobs of the dough.

Fill a saucepan one-third full of oil and heat to 200°C (400°F) – test with a frying thermometer. Drop the dough pieces into the hot oil and cook until a deep golden colour, about 4–6 minutes in total. (Flip them over with tongs as they cook.) Open one to test – the inside must be damply soft, not raw. Remove from the oil, drain on crumpled kitchen paper and keep hot while you cook the remainder.

To make the syrup, put the honey and lemon juice into a saucepan and heat until scented. Spoon over the fritters and sprinkle with ground cinnamon.

**1 sachet easy-blend dried yeast, 7 g**

**250 g plain flour, sieved**

**1 teaspoon sugar**

**½ teaspoon salt**

**corn or peanut oil, for deep-frying**

**4 teaspoons ground cinnamon, to serve**

HONEY SYRUP

**125 ml clear honey**

**juice of 1 lemon**

**MAKES ABOUT 20**

40 g ghee or unsalted butter

40 g white basmati rice, washed, drained and air-dried

2 fresh bay leaves, crushed

2 litres full-cream milk

100 g light muscovado sugar

75 g currants or raisins

12 green cardamom pods, crushed, black seeds removed, pods discarded

25 g pistachio or pine nuts or both

½ teaspoon rosewater or almond essence (optional)

1–2 sheets thin silver foil (varak) (optional, for special occasions)

SERVES 4

Put the ghee or butter into a large, wide, heavy-based, preferably non-stick 5 litre saucepan and heat gently until melted.

Stir-fry the rice until it darkens to pale gold, then add the bay leaves and milk. Increase the heat to high and, stirring constantly, bring to a frothing boil (about 10–12 minutes). Reduce the heat slightly to medium high.

Let the milk boil for another 35–40 minutes, until reduced to about half the original volume. Add the sugar, currants or raisins and cardamom. Continue to cook on a low heat, stirring often, for a further 15–20 minutes, until reduced to about a third or a quarter of its original volume. Stir and cool over iced water, then chill.

Decorate with nuts and silver foil, if using, lifting the foil on its attached tissue paper, inverting it over the pudding, then pulling off the amount needed using a fine brush. The pieces do not need to be immaculate – fragments look good.

# Indian rice pudding
## with cardamom and pine nuts

India is renowned for her superb condensed milk puddings and this one is wonderful served warm, cool or chilled. Cardamom, nuts, rosewater or almond essence, as well as sugar in various forms, add scent. For a special occasion, top it with varak, which is real silver, hand-beaten into paper-fine sheets. It is available from Asian shops or specialist grocers and adds drama to this already exotic dish.

I make few cakes and those I do make have to be quick, effortless and absolutely gorgeous. Serve slices with citrus sorbet as a pudding. Alternatively, enjoy it purely as a cake with a tiny espresso and a glass of iced water. Cointreau or Grand Marnier are excellent alternatives for the lemon liqueur.

# semolina citrus cake

Reserve a little of the shredded lemon and orange zest and put the remainder into a bowl with the oil, sugar, salt, orange and lemon juice and eggs. Whisk together with an electric or balloon whisk until light, smooth and well mixed.

Sieve the semolina and baking powder into a second bowl and add the ground almonds. Fold the almond essence and orange flower water into the egg mixture. Pour all at once into the dry ingredients and fold together, but do not overmix. Spoon into the prepared tin and smooth the top.

Bake towards the top of a preheated oven at 180°C (350°F) Gas 4 for 40–45 minutes or until pale gold at the edges and firm in the middle. A skewer pushed into the centre should come out clean.

Remove from the oven and let cool in the tin for about 10 minutes. Sprinkle the liqueur over the top. Push the cake out, still on its loose metal base, and let cool on a wire rack for another 10 minutes. Remove the base and paper. Serve in 8 or 12 wedges, warm or cool, but not chilled.

The cake will keep in an airtight container for up to 4 days.

**shredded or grated zest and juice of 1 lemon**

**shredded or grated zest and juice of 1 orange**

**185 ml extra virgin olive oil**

**215 g caster sugar**

**¼ teaspoon salt**

**3 medium eggs**

**200 g semolina**

**1 teaspoon baking powder**

**115 g ground almonds**

**1 teaspoon almond essence**

**1 teaspoon orange flower water**

**4 tablespoons Cointreau or Grand Marnier (or authentic Limuneddu liqueur)**

*a loose-based round cake tin, 23 cm diameter, lightly oiled and base-lined*

**SERVES 8–12**

This cake is made in less than ten minutes and baked in forty, so you get a spectacular result for little effort. It's made with olive oil, so you can soothe your conscience by telling yourself how healthy it is.

# greek honey, walnut and brandy cake

**125 ml extra virgin olive oil**

**100 g caster sugar**

**2 medium eggs**

**200 g walnut pieces**

**185 g self-raising flour, sieved**

**¼ teaspoon salt**

**125 ml strained plain Greek yoghurt or thick-set yoghurt**

**2 tablespoons brandy**

**2 tablespoons clear honey**

*a loose-based round cake tin, 20 cm diameter, oiled and base-lined*

**SERVES 8–12**

Put the oil, sugar and eggs into a large bowl and whisk with an electric beater until smooth and thick. Reserve a handful of the walnut pieces for decoration and chop the remainder with a knife or food processor in brief bursts until fine, but not mealy.

Add to the bowl, together with the flour, salt and yoghurt. Using broad strokes, mix the batter with a wooden spoon until smooth and even. Do not overmix.

Spoon the mixture into the prepared cake tin and smooth flat on top. Scatter with the reserved nuts.

Bake towards the top of a preheated oven at 190°C (375°F) Gas 5 for 40 minutes.

Test the centre – a skewer inserted at an angle into the centre should come out clean. Listen for a popping, bubbling sound, too.

Put the brandy and honey into a small bowl and stir until dissolved. Trickle the mixture over the top of the cake, then let cool in the tin for 20 minutes, still in the turned-off oven.

Remove the cake, still on its loose metal base, and cool on a wire rack for about 10 minutes. Remove the base, peel off the paper and serve warm or cold.

The cake will keep in an airtight container for 4 days.

# index